Praise for **Apples to Apples**

Apples to Apples is much more than theory and vague concepts.
it provides an easy-to-understand, common-sense approach—with
real-world examples of how other companies have solved their
problems—to identify, analyze, and deal with many of the tough
realities we face in business and industry today. Apples to Apples is
the kind of book that makes you want to take action right away. In
fact, before I was finished reading, and before I had a chance to order copies for my leadership team, I was emailing ideas culled from
its pages to my Business Development and Strategic Planning teams
as topics to discuss at our next leadership offsite.

> – *John J. Gallo,*
> *Executive Vice President, Rolls-Royce Corporation*

Dan Paulson writes from experience and common sense. He has
created a clear roadmap for any business that wants to be a Golden
Apple in a barrel of red ones which is what we all want to do with
our businesses. There are many specific ideas that Dan writes about
that I can see helping my business to be better. My guess is that you
will find the same. Well written and easily applicable.

> – *David Pauly*
> *CEO and Chairman Capitol Insurance Companies*

# Apples to **Apples**
## HOW TO STAND OUT FROM YOUR COMPETITION

by
Dan Paulson

First Person Productions   Madison, Wisconsin

Cover design by Todd Brei designbrei.com
Interior design by Sarah White

ISBN: 978-0-9844413-8-9

This book is available at special quantity discounts. The author is
available for consulting or speaking engagements.
www.invisionbusinessdevelopment.com
Twitter: InVision_brand
Facebook: InVision.business
Linkedin: linkedin.com/in/invisionu

USA:                          China:
P.O. Box 45920                Nankai District – Tianjin – China
Madison, WI  53744            www.growinchina.com
Phone: 608-467-0223

FIND US ON:

# Acknowledgements

When reflecting on the path to creating this book there are many who deserve credit and thanks. Life guides you down many roads and what you pick up along the way can come to define you. This book would not have been possible if my life had gone another direction. That is our own unique differentiator. Fortunately, my path has introduced me to some tremendous people, some of which I will name here.

First of all a special thanks goes out to my wife, Hope. She deals with my insanity and crazy ideas daily while caring for our two children. Without her support, I wouldn't be able to do the things I do.

Next I offer thanks for my children. I have been blessed with a couple of great kids who amaze me with their intelligence (and that they can be even more stubborn than me). I couldn't imagine my life without them.

My parents both deserve credit as well. They believed in me and continue to encourage me to this day.

Finally, thank you to all my clients and colleagues. Your feedback and your experiences have helped create this book and for that I am eternally grateful. Special thanks goes to Chip, Shari, Tracy, Andre, Rick, Lois, and Dave, my Mastermind partners and co-authors of the first book. They always challenge me to do better.

Here's wishing each of you great success.

# Contents

## PART 1
## The Need for Competitive Differentiation

## PART 2
## The Five Tasks of the Golden Apple

# PART 3
## Start Now

# Foreword

By John J. Gallo
Executive Vice President, Rolls-Royce Corporation

From my early days as a young manager working at Hormel, through successive leadership roles with GE, Piper Aircraft, and Rolls-Royce, I've read my share of management books and business articles to keep my skills sharp and to provide the fuel to help me and my companies improve, change, and grow continuously. Many of those books focused on a single-minded approach to improvement—whether it was by emphasizing quality, or excellence, or continuous improvement—or, to be less than diplomatic, the flavor of the moment. Dan Paulson's *Apples to Apples* is, however, uniquely different.

From the opening chapter, I found Dan's real world experiences and teachings compelling and applicable to the challenges my team and I face at Rolls-Royce. His multifaceted approach speaks to every business element and provides a wealth of knowledge, regardless of whether you are in sales, marketing, manufacturing, finance, quality or any other key business function. It very much provides one-stop-shopping for the tools and insights required for organizational and business change and growth.

In our fast-paced world, and with our equally fast-paced careers, it is easy to skim through a book and say "I don't need this" or "I know that." The strength of Dan's approach, however, is that it forces the reader to look in the mirror. His repeated challenge to identify what differentiates your business from the rest of the competition compelled me to dig into the realities of my business challenges, identify root causes and then implement corrective actions to drive improvement.

With *Apples to Apples,* I found myself using the book as a "time out" to slow down and analyze a number of dynamic situations.

Dan's innovative Reality Assessments made me take stock in ways that I hadn't before. By asking the right questions and using spot-on real world examples of success and how to overcome setbacks (Apple, Sony, and 3M are a few) he makes you reassess a lot of sacred paradigms. I especially appreciated his "Influencing Factors and Your Path" tool that I was able to use immediately to assess some thorny business issues and highlight areas that my leadership team and I needed to address.

*Apples to Apples* provides an easy-to-understand, common-sense approach—with real-world examples of how other companies have solved their problems—to identify, analyze, and deal with many of the tough realities we face in business and industry today.

*Apples to Apples* is the kind of book that makes you want to take action right away. In fact, before I was finished reading, I was emailing ideas culled from its pages to my Business Development and Strategic Planning teams as topics to discuss at our next leadership offsite.

My advice to anyone looking for that competitive edge and advantage is to take your time to really digest its lessons and apply Dan Paulson's approach exactly as he suggests: Don't skip any of it. Look in the mirror and drive change from your honest "Harsh Reality Assessments" to the Metrics he outlines to gauge improvement. Do that, and I am sure *Apples to Apples* will have the same impact on you and your business as it has on me and my business.

# PART 1

## The Need for Competitive Differentiation

## Using This Book

Throughout the book I will highlight important points and provide other resources for your learning.

*Know This:* These tips summarize critical points discussed throughout this book.

*Do This:* These tips convey action items you should put on your to-do list to utilize the concepts of this book.

These icons will help you find specific topics of interest:

Sales   Comm-  Leader-  Team-  Customer   Oper-  Branding   Goals
unication   ship   work   Service   ations

I have given labels to the Five Tasks of the Golden Apple, represented by these icons, which identify the chapters that deal specifically with each task:

Direction    Path    People    Process    Measures

Please pay attention to these icons and boxes. They will help you relate the material to your own challenges, and put into action the ideas and concepts you learn. There will also be references to a workbook that accompanies this book. If you haven't picked up the workbook yet, I recommend you do.

**Chapter**

# 1

# Introduction

The bankers needed help.

They were planning a retreat centered on marketing, and asked me to make a presentation. One of the topics they wanted to cover was product and service differentiation—how to do a better job of marketing. The organizers told me, "These banks find it difficult to separate themselves from their competition."

Not surprising. As with many businesses, most of the products the banks offer are the same. The services are also pretty close to identical and are usually communicated in general terms without truly describing what makes one bank's service different from another's. The only differentiating factor becomes rates—how much interest the customer would earn or pay and what sorts of service fees are involved. It comes down to a price-point issue. And I recognized the global economic downturn that began in 2008 makes exploring the whole question of price competition more urgent.

Of course, the trick in such a highly competitive market is to figure out what in your offerings, your culture, or your vision makes you different. How do you figure that out? That was the question the bankers were asking.

The 2008 Economic Crisis Made Differentiation a Crucial Issue

I was prepared to help the bankers discover a way to isolate their own special difference and market themselves. The economic crisis that hit all corners of our economy had already put me through my own search for differentiation. It had forced me as a business con-

> ### *Differentiation Equals Price Advantage.*
> **KNOW THIS**
>
> *Businesses that compete on products and services alone often battle over price. When a business has a clear point of difference, easily communicated to potential customers, the sale will likely be made on factors other than price. The clearly-differentiated company gains a price advantage, without having to cut prices.*

sultant to do some differentiating against both bigger companies and the little guys who were coming in and saturating the market.

When the economy is going well, consultants are busy. We can charge prices that allow us to support our margins and grow. But when there is a shift in the economy the "rules" change. The game changes. One of the changes I saw as companies began to shed employees was an increasing number of new competitors for my business.

News articles were telling people: "If you're laid off, you should go into business for yourself as a consultant." Oh, sure, that means inexperienced people who are unemployed and don't know the market will start thinking they can make a lot of money as a consultant. Established consultants, who had been out there charging $250 to $300 an hour for their services, now have to compete with these newcomers who think: "Gosh, I was making $30 or $40 or $50 an hour and I was doing pretty well on that—I'm going to come in at that price point. If I get a bunch of clients I'll be making a killing here."

Newcomers have just about saturated the market promising the same service, the $250-to-$300-an-hour consultants were offering, at a price that is 20 to 30 percent of what the current competitors charge.

The newcomers are all marketing to the same potential clients, offering the same services. The newcomers are hungry and they have to feed their kids and pay their mortgages, but they are not thinking about the number of clients they will need at that price point. They will run out of time and money before they cover their overhead. I don't care what business you're in, you still have a car payment, a mortgage payment, and insurance; you still have basic office needs to meet. These factors will eventually start eliminating competitors and lead to a correction. But for the short run the market is flooded with business consultants.

Any good business manager knows what is needed to break even and what is needed to be profitable. A flood of inexperienced low-balling competitors can undercut my established business by as much as half. It forced me to recalibrate what I was doing – how I was marketing myself and the types of clients I targeted.

Through internal analysis I determined that I don't want to work with everybody. I want to pick select client groups to go after, so I can wisely invest the money I put into self-marketing and end up with clients I like. This decision differentiates me from those consultants who say, "I'll take anybody." That means they have to target and sell themselves to "anybody." That's tough. Targeting anybody is targeting everybody, and that will dilute your appeal as you try to make it apply to a larger audience. Such an approach could only work if you can still keep your differentiation clear and handle the volume. But in reality most businesses are small. Many are at the micro-business level, one to ten employees. If you're at that level, scalability is even more difficult. Sellers of products or services don't usually achieve the scalability to serve "anybody" until they're huge.

### What Sets You Apart?

*This book will break the search for the answer to that question into components related to product, culture, marketing, and leadership. You will learn basic, consistent steps that help you apply these components in your search for the "thing" that differentiates your company. You will learn how to look at factors like marketing in a new way, to find and communicate the one clear message that gets people to understand what makes you different from the rest.*

KNOW THIS

## Depending on Price Differentiation Is Inadequate

If you are going to compete exclusively on price, your only alternatives are to find ways to make your product cheaper or your service faster and cheaper—something you should be doing anyway. But if price becomes the only differentiator, then the guy who undercuts the next guy will usually be the one who wins.

There is nothing wrong with becoming more cost-efficient and effective in your pricing, but if all you are going to do is focus on price, then that's all you have to compete on. A lot of businesses get themselves into a downward spiral of price competition and discounting that way, even those that are focusing on differentiation.

They say, "Our difference is in our products and our services." Again, using banks as an example—A bank competing on price might claim its difference is giving customers an extra quarter point interest on a deposit or lowering a half point on a loan. Many banks are streamlining and cutting back, and they have to watch their costs too. It's difficult to offer a price advantage significant enough to stand out without "breaking the bank." This is similar to manufacturing, in which the price of a widget is related to its cost of manufacture.

Unless there is a clear differentiation or a reason to buy based on features other than price, price becomes the driver of the purchase decision. That means your product or service has become "commoditized"—and you have to compete with anyone who has the power to undercut your pricing.

Eventually, when you no longer have the resources to compete, you are going to have to make very hard decisions. You will have to cut back. And where do most businesses usually cut back? All the training and development goes out the window because such things

**KNOW THIS**

### What it Means to Be "Commoditized"

To be "commoditized" is to be turned into a commodity— useful merchandise, but without distinctive features. A product becomes a commodity when customers perceive little or no value difference between brands or versions.

cannot be quantified. Then the business will have to tell its employees they're just going to have to do their jobs. "And oh by the way, we're going to expect you to be more creative and more productive than you were in the past." People will have to figure out how to do that, but without training. Such decisions launch a downward tumble, and soon the business is cutting deeper.

If that happens, you probably will have to start laying people off. You might restructure the company or let certain people go. But those lay-offs could incite more panic because the people who were not laid off will question the viability of the company and the security of their positions. They will be thinking, "I'm now doing my work plus John Smith's work—my workload's doubled and no one's told me how to prioritize. I'm not working smarter, just harder. And who knows if I'll be cut next!"

You now have the problem of increased stress among the workers, which in turn causes productivity to drop further. In short, when your only differentiation is price, you can very well end up on a slippery slope that compounds all your problems and results in instability.

## Price Competition Includes You in a Global Market

Depending on what your product or service is, you may be competing with organizations from anywhere in the world. And further, no matter what you offer, the Internet could now be your biggest headache. A huge market of potential customers has a cable modem or higher speed connection that allows them to transfer large amounts of information back and forth quickly. And e-commerce has developed into a trusted way of doing business; open to anyone who can set up the software.

Conversely, anybody with a computer, an Internet connection, and something to sell can now sell it to someone down the street and someone on the other side of the world. Today businesses of every size are competing on a world scale. The potential advantage to the competitors is that it's cost-effective to reach out to a larger audience. Where once only very large companies could afford to compete at that level, now the Internet makes it possible for smaller businesses to do so as well. Of course, from the point of view of each competitor, whatever they're selling will also be sold by many more businesses operating from locations that could be anywhere. Location may not even matter anymore.

The problem with this very large number of competing sellers is that every business is pushed toward competing primarily on price. And it's harder to maintain a premium price when you may be competing with countries where price is based on a totally different cost structure.

Depending on the types of products or services you offer, you could be affected by global competition. So far, for example, the biggest impact from global competition has been to services that require larger groups of people to collaborate on a project, such as the information technology and telephony fields. Software engineering often requires many people writing code and programming parts of the software. In this case the product is information—how information is generated, tracked, and manipulated. India has jumped to the forefront of this field in the last decade. China too. According to some sources it appears these companies have access to a more highly-educated workforce than the U.S. does. In fact, depending on the statistics cited, the number of honor students in China or India is greater than the total number of students in the U.S. And both Indian and Chinese cultures already place high value on science and mathematics.

There is now a knowledge glut in these countries. They are able to work for pennies on the dollar and do essentially what a company in the U.S. would. And further, many of their employees have come

**KNOW THIS**

### *Understand Globalization*
*All companies should understand how globalization will impact them.*

> ### *You Must Stand Out*
> *What part of your product or service is general, commoditized, readily available anywhere? And on the other hand, what is it that your business has that is not commoditized—that is specific to you? Your answer might center on your culture and your people, and how you use that to differentiate your business from the rest. The answer doesn't have to be high-tech. It can be low-tech—the nature of your communication, the efficiency with which you work. What will set you apart from your competition? That's what you have to figure out.*

*KNOW THIS*

to the U.S. for higher education. They speak English, and are familiar with U.S. culture. Because of different living standards and monetary conversions, Chinese and Indian firms are able to be highly competitive on price. Price-conscious clients may see this as a way to save money. Clearly, unless you are willing to compete globally, you stand to lose a lot.

Whether you are competing globally or not, you need a strategy to lift you out of the vicious cycle of price competition. You need to explore this simple question: **How do you do something different enough that your consumers or clients will quickly recognize and understand that difference?**

## Escaping Price Competition Is The Key to Differentiation

Every purchase is an emotional purchase. The emotion might be indifference—that's still an emotion. Think about it—every purchase you make, of a product or service, is driven by your emotions. How did the seller trigger your emotions so you made the decision to buy that particular product or service?

People are primarily motivated to buy by two factors—pleasure and pain. A business has to offer products or services that reduce pain, increase pleasure, or do both.

### The "Pleasure or Pain Principle" in Action

I was referred to a fee-for-service dental practice that was quite specialized in its approach to dentistry. That unique approach to pain management was their differentiator, but it was difficult for people to understand just how that helped them versus the approach a typical dentist would take. The dentists in this practice needed to learn how to talk about what they did in a way their customers could understand.

I coached them to get the message right by focusing on the "pleasure or pain principle." Most of their patients were in pain. Too often, that pain was not being adequately managed in the traditional health care practices. The patients had followed all recommendations, but their pain had not gone away.

So this practice was a stop of last resort, in a way. I needed to convey to that dentist and his staff how to get the patient to understand the potential to move away from pain (for the first time in a long time, in some cases) and why it was worth the investment. It would not be covered by insurance in many cases; a price factor that made convincing a potential patient a unique challenge. The dentists had to comprehend the pleasure and pain principle as a motivating factor. "This is how I'm going to get back to feeling the way I truly want to feel." That is the message we spent time on. As a result, we were able to make some remarkable changes in that practice over a relatively short time. Execution on new messaging that conveyed their unique difference, with an emotional impact that really appealed to potential patients, was the strategy that succeeded for that dental practice.

This could be your key to differentiation—knowing how to direct your offering at a real pain people are feeling, and communicating how your product is going to reduce their pain —or better yet, how it will move them from pain to pleasure. Remember, however, once your product is producing pleasure, you will have to keep customers happy and assure they don't go back from pleasure to pain!

Whether you focus on what is unique about your product, or what is unique about your service, look for the emotions that drive the purchase. That will put you on the trail of the answer to the question driving this book: How do you do something different enough that the consumer will understand what that difference is? You may find the answer by studying how your offering changes pain to pleasure.

### The Advantage of Creating a Fan Base

KNOW THIS

With a good "pain to pleasure" message, you can leverage your clients and prospects to create the kind of fan base that worships the ground you walk on. They will even wait in line for hours on end to get your product or service. Once people understand the value of a specific offering, and what exactly makes it unique, they are more willing to wait, more forgiving of mistakes, and more likely to refer business.

### Your Differentiator is the Key to Branding

This book approaches branding from a perspective you probably have not seen before. It takes a holistic look into business and culture and can help you understand the variables that impact the growth of your business. The book breaks down culture and branding into its raw materials and gives you some tools you can put to use immediately. There is also a workbook that follows the text, and I highly recommend using this tool as you seek to transform your business. Last, but not least, the book provides links to online resources that you can use as a reference. So let's get started...

## Chapter

# 2

# Competitive Differentiation: It's No Joke

I once heard a comedian say, "I want to be different just like everyone else!" As business leaders, each of us probably sees ourselves in that statement. We want to be familiar to our customer and yet we wish to be different enough that we stand out. As you know this is no easy feat.

To be different involves figuring out what truly separates us. What makes us unique. We may even hire someone to help us out. These experts ask us a few questions and formulate what they call a "brand." This image is created in our likeness. It involves a new logo, color scheme, a story, a marketing campaign and quite possibly a large estimate for the work they will do. We negotiate, we invest, and we wait. If marketing has done a good job, we might see a positive change in sales. If they miss, we find ourselves with thousands less in the bank account and no increased sales to speak of. Worse, if misaligned, it can lead to short-term gain and long-term pain.

Throughout my career, I have heard this story time and time again. Businesses hand over the keys to the kingdom and have someone else create their identity, try to make them unique, and the return on investment is hardly measurable in most cases. Now, I am not saying there are not good marketing agencies out there. Actually, there are a lot of very talented people who, with the right information, can help you communicate your brand. What you need to remember is that logo, colors and advertising are all superficial.

**KNOW THIS**

## *Customers Know...*

*Know what truly makes you different. Start by asking your customer, "What is it about us?"*

In order to be successful they must align with what your business actually is.

Most of us don't realize what makes us different. Often we focus our differences on product, price or service. Unless you are the only company in your market, none of these will define you completely. I have heard various sources make the comment, "In order for you to truly differentiate yourself, you are either the best, or you are the cheapest. If you cannot claim either of these, then you are just like everybody else."

I agree with that statement; if you can't claim to be the best—at least in your market—or the cheapest, you haven't figured out what really makes you different. You are differentiating on product and service features, which means that when you do go into comparisons, it's hard not to be price-driven. That leads to commoditization. And that is a painful place to be.

**KNOW THIS**

## *Control the Message*

*Know your culture before you let someone else define it. You control the outcomes of your business. The wrong message will do nothing for you in the long term.*

When consumers move toward making a purchase decision, they begin with the "whether"—whether or not to buy. This is the yes/no, either/or decision that precedes the selection of an alternative. "Should I buy a new computer? Should I go to more conferences in my field?" This is where the "pleasure or pain" principle comes into play. As I said in the Introduction, people are primarily motivated to buy by their desire to move away from pain and toward pleasure.

They seek products or services that remove pain, deliver pleasure, or better yet, both.

The consumer weighs pros and cons—possibilities for pleasure or pain—and if the pros outweigh the cons, moves on to the "which." Consumers research available options, and quickly figure out the criteria the purchase must meet. "How much RAM should that new computer have? Which conferences are really relevant to my business?"

Consumers get recommendations from trusted friends, use on-line research, and so on, until they have created for themselves a decision set—a group of specific offerings, from specific vendors that appear to measure up to the desirable criteria they have defined.

Now the consumer must make a choice of one alternative from the decision set. This is where your opportunity to be the provider of choice emerges. At this point, you are "different just like everybody else"—everybody in the decision set, that is. It's critical to your success that you stand out in that decision set as the offering most likely to wow on more of the criteria than any other hopeful.

---

### Do Your Customers Like You?

*How much of your business comes from referrals? Check your assumptions—don't let your gut be your guide on this one. Take a quick trip through your client list or at least a random sample of your customers. If referrals are not the source of a good percentage of your customer base, you are probably commoditized more than you think. It's important to measure referrals, and work toward increasing that percentage.*

---

### An Honest Self-Evaluation

To move toward differentiation on truly meaningful dimensions, rather than being different "just like everybody else," begin by completing the Reality Assessment No. 1 in Figure 1.

*Figure 1*

## Harsh Reality Assessment No. 1: Your Market Position

*Answer the following 10 questions. If there are any you would like to answer as a maybe, make it a "No." (If you have to guess, the answer is probably "No" anyway.)*

1.  *I am perceived as the undisputed leader in my industry.*
    ____Yes ____No
2.  *We set the standards for our industry and others follow.*
    ____Yes ____No
3.  *Our staff is the best in the industry and we are recognized publicly for it.*
    ____ Yes ____No
4.  *We are highly profitable and can demand higher rates.*
    ____Yes ____No
5.  *Our company has a highly productive team.*
    ____Yes ____No
6.  *Our company manages change far better than our competition.*
    ____Yes ____No
7.  *Everyone in our company understands our Vision.*
    ____Yes ____No
8.  *Everyone in our company knows our strategic objectives.*
    ____Yes ____No
9.  *Everyone in our company understands the role they play in achieving our business initiatives.*
    ____Yes ____No
10. *We are not considered the best, but we are the cheapest and profitable because of it.*
    ____Yes ____No

To determine your score on Reality Assessment No. 1, total the questions you answered "Yes."

How did you do? Did you score at least a 5? Did you score fewer? If you are not considered the industry leader, are you at least the cheapest? No? Most companies would not score well here. To be fair, these questions are asked at a global scale. You may be the leader in your industry, but that may only extend to your town, state or region. The other questions are more relevant no matter what size you are.

If your score on this assessment falls between 3 and 8, then you are in the same spot as more than 80 percent of the businesses out there. And if you are feeling your market shrinking and competition increasing, these ten questions may help explain why.

You are probably thinking to yourself, "But how can you say this? The questions asked do not relate to my marketing." The fact is there are many variables that affect a business. Reality Assessment No. 1 dealt with your place in the market. You are either a leader or a follower. Business leaders find ways to be profitable through innovation and/or price. Followers spend most of their time worrying about what their competition is doing. Knowing your competition is important, but finding ways to leap past them is even more important. Otherwise, you are like the many businesses, stuck trying to play the game of catch-up.

If you are not a leader, chances are you are trying to be different, but getting pulled back in with the rest of your competition while a few visionaries move out ahead of the pack. To survive you have to grow.

Growth is achieved through people and change. First, let's look at how change brings growth—if it's carried out effectively, that is.

## Change Must be More than Skin Deep

To make my point about fundamental change versus change that is skin-deep only, let me start with the example of a building. Say you built a new office building. The day it's completed it looks fabulous. All the features are modern, it smells fresh; it reflects the latest style. But time passes. Tenants move in and out. Technology changes. The utilities age and little is done to care for the façade or interior.

Over time, your nice, new building starts looking less than desirable. New tenants are hard to find. You grow concerned because a building that was once making money now is costing you.

**KNOW THIS**

### *Start from Within*

*Before changing the look, you need to define what it is you want your business to become: what will it look like in one, five or ten years from now? Be sure to read Chapter 4, about vision.*

Then you come up with an idea. You hire a contractor to completely fix up the outside of the building. Because you aren't making money any more, you choose to spend all your money on the outside. You allow the contractor to do what he wants to your building just as long as he makes it nice again. He asks a few questions and gets to work creating a whole new look. The contractor does a wonderful job. When he's done, the building looks brand new from the street. Once again, tenants are attracted—until they go inside. Outside they see a modern building that is clean and fresh. Inside they see a building that is in desperate need of repair.

You might think it would be crazy to do that with a building. But in fact, that's what many companies do—make skin-deep changes, freshening their "façade" by changing advertising campaigns. It comes about like this—sales are going down. A few attempts are made to change the direction the business is headed, but due to concerns about expenses, they are done on the cheap. When the fixes do not work, advertising seems like the best option. So they "slap a new coat of paint on the old building"—they come up with some fresh advertising copy, maybe a new logo and brand elements. The business image appears fresh and updated, but when the customers come in, they experience the same old business that drove them away in the first place.

A company currently "getting change right" as I am writing this is Domino's Pizza. They dealt with a product problem and communicated about it well. In a recent ad campaign they have used the fact that they were rated so poorly to justify changes. They brought in focus groups to talk about pizza quality, and used comments and video from the focus groups that were very critical of the pizza. Instead of downplaying that criticism, they embraced it. "You are right, and we are going to make changes. And here are the changes we will make, based on the information you gave us." They faced it head-on and told the market to try the new product for themselves. And it's working out favorably so far. The latest twist is that they are asking customers to submit their own pizza photos to be used

### Logos and Advertising are Just the Facade

*KNOW THIS*

*The truth is the logo, colors and advertising are just the façade to your business. They are part of the brand, but not its core. Your brand is so much more than a logo, yet most people are led to believe that the look encompasses the entire brand.*

in future advertising. They are encouraging customers to drive the change that will make them grow.

Similarly, Microsoft has done a good job with Windows 7. There was bashing before it came out, especially because the previous launch of Vista was not well-accepted. Microsoft has to overcome years and years of expectation that each new release will just be a new headache. There is a consumer community talking about the product separate from the advertising messages, and they are skeptical about Windows.

So Microsoft came up with their "I am a PC" campaign. They used actors to stage little reenactments of ordinary people experiencing specific product benefits, like drag-and-drop interaction or start-up time. They have done a good job of playing up past weaknesses and showing how they have overcome them. That is communicating in a meaningful way, "Here is the pain you gave me, how are you bringing me back to pleasure?" That is a concept that has led to effective advertising messages for Microsoft.

Domino's and Microsoft have used advertising to grow their business with messages about change. That is an option for you if you are a national brand too. But most of our businesses are not at that scale. "We will cut back on these other areas and spend more on advertising" is not an option. You would be happy if more advertis-

**KNOW THIS**

*Learn Before You Spend*

*Even if you have millions to spend on marketing, there's a lot you can learn to make your marketing more effective. This book will help, and contacting us can help you learn more.*

ing would produce more name recognition and that would produce more business—but for most of us, it won't.

Most businesses do not have enough money to advertise enough to drive business forward that way. Even if you are running a multi-billion-dollar publicly-traded company, with millions to spend on advertising, its effectiveness is trending down. For too many companies advertising is not producing results the way it once did. There are a lot of other ways you could spend that money in your business and drive change more effectively. Instead of hiring marketing experts to launch new brands, hoping that will drive more business, look to your people. People make change happen. Your people have more impact on your company's growth than advertising dollars can.

## Your People Are Your Brand

Here's the secret very few will tell you. Your people are your brand. All businesses are people businesses. I don't care whether you are a tech company or a small town restaurant. People are the driving force behind every business. They build the company culture. The company culture dictates the direction the business will go. The better your people are at performing their roles and adapting as those roles change; and the better your leaders are at visioning, growth and communication; the stronger your business will be.

I have worked with many different companies throughout my career. It always amazed me how two almost identical companies in the same industry could perform so differently. Over the past few years I have had the pleasure of working with a number of dental practices. These practices have been great referral sources for me and at one point, I was working with three practices that were literally within blocks of each other. My primary role is to coach and advise and because I would be referred by the dentist down the road, there was little concern about competitive secrets being shared. To tell the truth all of the dentists were good at what they did. The financial performance of their practices would vary greatly. To an observer they all did the same things for their patients. They provided a similar process for treatment plans, similar follow up, similar care. Yet the revenue was very different.

There were many reasons why a dentist would hire me, but these reasons were often lumped into two categories. First, high-performing dentists would hire me because they wanted to be even more successful. They knew their limitations and they wanted to work through those challenges and enhance their practices. Second, under-performing dentists would hire me because they were not doing as well as they knew they should. Costs were going up, patients were going down, and the practice seemed to be stalling out. But

> ### *Measure "Employee Delight"*
> *What do your employees say about you? Every day your staff is marketing your business. Are they happy to be there? Do they convey that to your customers? What metrics do you have in place to measure "employee delight"?*
>
> **KNOW THIS**

how could this be? They all did the same thing. The way they did their work was very similar. The difference? It was in the people.

One practice I worked with was highly successful before I got there. The dentist did an amazing amount of business out of an office the size of a shoebox. It was small and cramped with people constantly tripping over each other, and it was BUSY! Once you met the staff you knew why. It was a fun place to be. Most people would not think of a visit to their dentist as a fun place, but the people working there enjoyed it. The patients coming in for their appointments felt welcomed and relaxed in an environment where people were smiling and laughing.

Now, it wasn't all fun and games. The staff worked in a fast-paced environment. The dentist was kind and focused. He was willing to share in the success of the practice. There were still challenges, disagreements, and conflicts, but the staff was able to work through these issues and move on. They were rewarded with solid

**KNOW THIS**

### Empower Your Employees
*Empowered employees are happier, more innovative, and less likely to leave.*

growth before I started working with the doctor and have grown even more since.

Another practice, a short distance away, was a different story. The practice was a nice sized office with a lot of modern features. The dentist was skilled and personable. Yet business had been even or on the decline for several years. Patients sat quietly in a large waiting room while staff members worked behind a large glass wall. The pace was different. It was quieter and slower. The staff was very pleasant, but the energy just wasn't the same. Price increases helped take some of the sting out of the slow growth, but eventually that wasn't able to keep revenues going. This office was more concerned about survival than growth and you could feel it.

Whether I am called in to work with a high-performing firm on generating even more success, or to help an under-performing firm turn that trend around, I find that my work almost always involves assessing and improving the contributions staff are making to the company culture.

To measure the effect of your staff are having on your ability to achieve competitive differentiation, complete the Reality Assessment in Figure 2.

## Figure 2

### Harsh Reality Assessment No. 2: Your Staff

*Answer the following questions. Again, if there are any you would like to answer as a maybe, mark it "No."*

1. *As a leader I have a clear vision.*
   ____Yes ____No
2. *My staff knows the expected results and is given the power to work towards them.*
   ____Yes ____No
3. *Our turnover is low.*
   ____ Yes ____No
4. *Our customers regularly rave about how great our people are.*
   ____Yes ____No
5. *Our staff enjoys coming to work.*
   ____Yes ____No
6. *When we have to hire, it's easy to find people.*
   ____Yes ____No
7. *I can ask any member of my team and they will know how they are performing on the job.*
   ____Yes ____No
8. *My staff actively works to make this a better place.*
   ____Yes ____No
9. *We are innovative because of the applied knowledge of our people.*
   ____Yes ____No
10. *Investing in my staff creates a measurable return in my business.*
    ____Yes ____No

Total the number of questions you answered with a "Yes" as you did with Reality Assessment No.1. Are the results any different? If not, why? A strong business with a culture of solid leadership, focused goals, and a capable staff would answer most of these questions positively. Seven "Yes" questions will get you a 'C' average and you are doing OK with room to improve. Any fewer and you are probably experiencing high turnover and/or an under-utilized staff.

People are such an important part of the business. Many companies acknowledge that, but are often afraid to invest in people and strategy when times are tight. In their minds it is a risk. The perception is you cannot measure performance. And to be honest, many companies spend money on strategy and training that only fail in the end. It is easy to understand why a leader would look at the people investment and want to cut back. After all, consultants will tell you that organizational development is measurable, but they may not show you how.

Also, businesses wait too long before addressing critical issues within their company. When times are good they are too busy selling and hiring to worry about addressing internal problems that may seem benign at the time. Unfortunately, it is those little problems that explode into larger ones when the business goes south.

## Differentiate Yourself or Your Customers Will

Everybody makes choices when it comes to purchasing decisions: first the "whether" followed by the "which." Sometimes the "which" is simple and sometimes it becomes quite complex. Many variables and contingencies factor in. But remember this; in the end the decision to buy is seldom made on price alone. Price becomes the deciding factor only after the customer's decision set is firmed up, and then only when the customer cannot easily distinguish any other difference between brands. When this happens the customer uses price as the final differentiator. In some cases (though rare) the consumer may actually choose the higher-priced item, because of the perception that "if you pay more, you are paying for quality." In most cases, however, consumers will seek out the lowest price for goods and services when they cannot differentiate one from another.

Time for the final Reality Assessment: How are you perceived by your customers? Complete the Reality Assessment in Figure 3.

**Figure 3**

### Harsh Reality Assessment No. 3: Customers

*Answer the following questions. Again, if the answer feels like a "maybe," mark it "No."*

1. *I generate a high percentage of business through referral.*
   _____ Yes _____ No
2. *We are constantly battling customers over price.*
   _____ Yes _____ No
3. *Our employees find little difference between us and our competitors.*
   _____ Yes _____ No
4. *Price is our least common differentiator.*
   _____ Yes _____ No
5. *Our customers talk positively about us online.*
   _____ Yes _____ No
6. *We are recognized by third parties (local/national media) as an industry leader.*
   _____ Yes _____ No
7. *We spend little money on marketing through traditional methods.*
   _____ Yes _____ No
8. *We rarely have to negotiate price with our clients.*
   _____ Yes _____ No
9. *We close a high percentage of prospects (greater than 60 percent).*
   _____ Yes _____ No

---

In Reality Assessment No. 3, if you answered "No" to more than five of the questions, you probably feel as though you are commoditized. This is the painful place of the middle, the B student and the "good enough" who never gets to be great. You are neither the best, nor the cheapest. You are left to haggle it out in the middle of the pack with competitors fighting for the same sale. If you answered more than five of these questions positively, your customers think well of you. You might still be feeling a pinch in some areas, but you are among the companies with the greatest opportunity to leverage customer goodwill to make a positive impact on business growth.

As a business leader, your primary responsibility is to create the conditions that make today's consumer want to connect with you, and with your company. It's the relationships you build that will build your business. Through your customers' connection with your people they make a choice to differentiate you.

When your customers choose you, again and again, for reasons other than price, you are not "different just like everyone else"—you are truly unique and valued as such.

**Chapter**

# 3

# The Pitfalls of Failing to Differentiate, And How to Avoid Them

Imagine for a moment that you are in an electronics store, comparing television sets, as I was just the other day.

I purchased my first HDTV in the early 2000s. At the time it was about the largest (50") and the highest resolution (1080i). I did not get a flat panel because they had just come on the market, and started at about $4,000 to $5,000 for the cheap ones. Back then, your selection was fairly limited and a decent TV would cost you at least $2,500.

Fast forward to today. The choices are endless and the technology is changing so rapidly that your set is out of date the moment you take it out of the store.

The advantage to all this change is that you get a lot of TV for your money. Sets are getting larger and cheaper, and there are many choices. On my recent visit to a big box store I saw hundreds of sets available—starting at 50 inches! Back when I was last shopping for a TV, resolution was the most important feature on which you could make comparisons. Now there are 3D TVs and Net TVs, LCDs, LEDs, Plasmas, and the list goes on. I consider myself a bit of a tech head and I still cannot keep up with all the changes. Worst of all, when I was staring at all those sets, I was left baffled about which one would truly serve me best. There were brands I recognized and brands I didn't. Some of the brands I considered "junk" twenty years ago are rated high-end brands today. With all the selection before me, I was left with only one choice: Go home and put off TV-shopping for another day.

All joking aside, having seen all those competing TV products and knowing the speed at which their technology is changing, I am more than willing to wait until the prices drop even further.

Many electronics products, televisions among them, have become commodity items, merchandise without meaningful differences between one product and another. That's an advantage to consumers—items that were once out of the price range of the masses are now affordable and in some cases even cheap. But that's the nature of the business, right? With innovation and growth come lower prices and commoditization. That may be the nature of the business, but for many companies, it is a sign of trouble, which brings me to the first pitfall.

## Pitfall No. 1: Trying to Appeal Too Broadly

One of the greatest mistakes we make as business leaders is to attempt to be the generalists in our industry. We fall under the false notion that if what we offer appeals to more people, we will get more business. But that can backfire. When what we offer appeals to a broad market, we risk our customers losing touch with who we are and what makes us different. That broad appeal, instead of creating more opportunity for sales, only creates more confusion.

You can probably call to mind a business that asserts in general terms that its products or services are different. "We have great service" or "our quality is the best" are two of the most overused claims of differentiation. Whether I am speaking to a group of people at a seminar or one-on-one with a business owner, I often get similar responses when I ask the question, "What makes you different?" Almost every time someone will say, "Well, nobody has better prod-

**KNOW THIS**

### *Focus or Else!*
*Trying to be all things to all people equals "nothing to no one."*

ucts than we do, and we have the best customer service." When I ask them to be more specific, I seldom get a satisfactory answer.

People need to know why your product or service is different. They need to know how your offering will help them. They need to know what the return on their investment will be, either realized or perceived. Businesses that use those needs to develop a clear message aimed at a specific group of potential customers avoid the pitfall of trying to appeal too broadly.

## Pitfall No. 2: Stuck in "Me Too"

Another pitfall of failing to differentiate on any aspect other than price is allowing others to drive your business strategy, rather than taking the lead. You can be "me too" in terms of the features you offer or in terms of the culture you create in your company. Both spring from your people.

How do your people make your company "me too" or help it avoid that trap? What do people have to do with being able to charge more, make more, and have a better brand?

Well, for starters, every business is created by people and run by people. People created the product, developed it, marketed it, made sure it met quality standards, and stood behind it. People innovated

---

### Innovate to Differentiate

*Innovative companies look for ways to leapfrog competitors, not just catch up with them. Define where you want to take your business that is different from competitors. Know what they do, but focus on what you do.*

KNOW THIS

---

the product to make it better or designed something totally new. People made the plant and office efficient, stayed up late, worked weekends, and did what they needed to do to make it successful. They gave the product a voice and breathed life into it. It was through the ingenuity and enthusiasm of those people that products and services were sold. It's the human factor that makes great companies great.

By the same token, people are also what bring companies down. Poor leadership, lack of vision, lack of direction, unwillingness to change, complacency, failure to recognize problems and address them, over-promising and under-delivering, arrogance, failure to address competition, denial, and focusing on short-term gains over long-term are just some of the problems that stem from people. These are the human factors that lead to poor company performance and the pitfall of becoming commoditized. (You will notice many of these are failures on the leaders' part, as opposed to the employees'.)

I have listened to plenty of business leaders say, "Our difference is our people." So how do you communicate that in your advertising in a meaningful way? If you do not find a specific, believable, way to make that point, you are still stuck with a "me too" position. And that means you are commoditized.

Promotions for commoditized products typically focus on how they are like their competition. The compare-and-contrast message is about showing how competitor A's product is really no different than competitor B's. Often the only difference demonstrated is price. "If all options are basically the same, the smart money is on the cheapest," the message goes.

To avoid being "me too" you will have to do the research in your own business to determine what really makes you different. If you are claiming quality and service set you apart, then you have got plenty of competitors saying the same thing. Failure to communicate specific, meaningful differentiators is the primary factor that leads to commoditization.

---

**KNOW THIS**

**$**

### *Two Reasons Sales are Lost*

*When you lose out to your competition because of price it is for one of two reasons:*

1. *Your prospect/client did not believe that the other service or product was that much different from yours, or*
2. *Your prospect/client did not have the confidence that your service or product was indeed better and worth the extra investment.*

If a person in the market for what you sell cannot determine why your product or service is better than the other guys', then that potential buyer's decision becomes just a matter of price. Price will speak until performance proves otherwise.

You have probably had this experience—choosing the lower cost item, and then finding glaring deficiencies popping up. But that is after the fact. Another business with better quality and a higher price failed to convince the buyer that its better quality was worth the extra cost. That business has lost the sale—and the revenue. That business could be you—unless you avoid the "me too" pitfall.

---

### Complacency Can Kill a Leader

*We all talk about how good we are, but do we back it up? The lead you think you have can be taken away by a competitor who capitalizes on your weaknesses. If you fail to sustain your leadership position, you'll soon pay the price. Instead of being too busy to keep up with the volume, you'll be busy keeping up with the competition—falling right back into "me too" and Pitfall No. 2.*

**KNOW THIS**

---

As a business leader, you have to figure out ways to address those problem points up-front. Research should help you ask questions about your own business that go beyond quality and service, to clarify *why*. Find answers that allow you to say, "This is what we mean by quality, and this is why our quality is different." Or, "This is what we mean by service, and this is why our service is different." Now you are not "me too"—you are "different, wow!"

Remember the "pleasure or pain" principle—people seek products or services that remove pain, deliver pleasure, or better yet, both. What can you say to your consumers that convey the message that the specific way you are different is worth a higher price, because the purchase moves from pain toward pleasure?

## Pitfall No. 3: Always Being Stuck in the "Lowest Price"

In this variation on the "me too" pitfall, other companies are driving your pricing decisions. They're in charge of the price points

**KNOW THIS**

### Differentiation Equals Price Advantage.

*Businesses that compete on products and services alone often battle over price. When a business has a clear point of difference, easily communicated to potential customers, the sale will likely be made on factors other than price. The clearly-differentiated company gains a price advantage, without having to cut prices.*

you can charge—you're stuck with "Their price minus 10 percent."

If you cannot differentiate yourself on other compelling features, potential customers will say, "I'm going with Brand X because they're charging 20 percent less than you are." You battle on price. You cannot get off that factor to move toward the true differentiators.

The television story that opened this chapter is a very simplis-

**KNOW THIS**

### Find the Right Fit

*Are you willing to walk away from a potential sale? Can you turn down business when it's not the right fit? If you are prospecting properly, you can. Pre-qualify to find your right fit and avoid wasting time on customers who won't value you.*

tic example of commoditization at work. In reality every industry will face commoditization at some point. Legal Zoom now provides services for a few hundred dollars that would cost thousands with lawyers. QuickBooks made it easier for business people to enter their own accounting information instead of hiring a bookkeeper or accountant. IT consultants are now sourced from other countries where the talent is high and the labor is cheap. It seems only natural that price should be driven down when commoditization increases.

> ### *Doing Business at the Bottom of the Bell Curve*
> *Sometimes being the cheapest works as a business strategy. When you are dealing with economies of scale, sheer volume can make up the difference and lead to profitability. If that describes your business, what's the chance that someone can beat your price and match quality? If the answer is yes, "there is a good chance," you are vulnerable. It is time to look for more meaningful differentiators.*

KNOW THIS

When markets become highly competitive there is a natural tendency to compete on price. After all, price is the easiest differentiator. It is an objective measure and it's natural for people to look at price when considering purchases. Many business owners fall into this pitfall. Competitors lower their prices and pretty soon most of the businesses follow. What choice do they have? Comparison shoppers force the point: If the products or services are equivalent, then the prices should be as well.

In fact, there is often a wide range of prices for any product or service. Typically pricing follows a model similar to a bell curve. There is a mid-range price for an item, and 80 percent of comparable offerings' prices will fall within one standard deviation of that mean price. In addition, there will be a few outliers. Some prices fall well below the mean while others soar well above. Wouldn't you rather be at the upper end, charging a premium price, and enjoying greater profitability? While many businesses strive to be on the upper end of the bell curve, most will fail. Those that succeed do so because they have communicated a point of difference that is more valuable than money to a particular target market.

If you want to stop letting others drive your price you'll have to stop thinking about price and start thinking about fit. You need to be perceived as a good fit in order to get beyond the price factor. So what are ways you can make sure your company—and the product or service you offer—are a good fit for your potential buyer?

**DO THIS**

### *Develop a Growth Plan*

*Is fast growth always good growth? That depends. What are you building the business for? The answer may make slow, steady growth preferable to a fast rise. Determine what organizational needs will be filled and when, based on the speed, you intend to grow. What happens if it's faster than planned? Slower? Plan for these important "what-ifs."*

These aspects of "fit" are driven by your company culture:

- Alignment of core ideas/beliefs
- Lower staff turnover
- Signs of innovation and growth, especially in difficult times
- Constant communication through multiple channels in your organization
- Testimonials from other clients
- Having a "giving" mentality, meaning you are client-centered and always concerned with helping them increase their bottom line, solve a problem, or be more efficient.

As consumers, we all want to find the best fit for our needs. As business leaders, we can escape the pitfall of "lowest price" by exploiting that. When your people are helping you sell on fit, rather than price, you'll close more sales. You can move out from behind the "lowest price" pitfall and start leading from your true core strengths.

## Pitfall No. 4: Failing to Capitalize on the Position of Undisputed Leader

All business leaders would prefer that their businesses be perceived as the best in their industry. Let's face it, people want to be associated with winners, in terms of what they create, where they work, and what they buy.

A company that enjoys a position of undisputed leadership can become complacent. This pitfall tends to happen with businesses that initially had little competition and so, gained large market share. Those companies remind me of the book fable of The Tortoise and The Hare. Though the hare was much quicker, he was too confident in his skills. In the end, the slow and steady tortoise won the race because of the hare's overconfidence.

Being on top can create a false sense of security. Companies that are doing well can neglect to take care of the little issues that get in the way of business growth. It may be that they hire people but fail to fully train them or they fail to address operational issues because of work volume. A company that is climbing fast can become so confident it goes into a coasting mode. What looks like success is really just a focus on handling the demand of today without any focus on tomorrow.

Where there is a company complacent in its leadership position, there can also be arrogance. The company may fall into complacency due to lack of competition over the years. These companies may be highly successful, in spite of neglecting to take care of basic issues, simply because they remained unchallenged in their niche. They succeed until their market shifts or competition begins to erode away sales. The company that fails to notice and respond to that shift is in danger of a painful fall into Pitfall No. 4.

## To Avoid Pitfalls, Embrace Change

Appealing too broadly; letting competitors set the agenda; pricing lower than low; failing to hold the lead when you have it—any of these pitfalls can sidetrack your business growth. These pitfalls can be avoided—but not if you don't do something to address their dangers.

In truth many leaders are aware of these challenges and yet fail to take action. Why could this be? A big part of the failure to act is the fact that people and processes will need to change. For many people "change" is a scary word. People believe change is hard, extra work, painful, and prone to failure. That is a common perception. The reality is; "Change is continually going on around us, and it is our failure to change that gets us into trouble."

**DO THIS**

### *Encourage Questions*

*Teach your people to always ask questions. Never settle for "that's the way it's always been." Support people who challenge ideas in a productive way by encouraging new concepts and then building upon those ideas to make them better.*

Up to this point I have shared with you the advantages of differentiation along with the potential pitfalls. If you have been in business for long, on some level, you probably already knew something about these advantages and risks. We all know there is danger out there for every business that fails to stand out from its competition.

So let's move forward. I will provide you a way to distinguish yourself from your competition, but not through traditional methods you might find in other books that talk about branding. Here we are going to peel back the layers to expose the deepest workings of your business. From this point we will begin building a brand from the inside out, a brand based on the very core of your company culture.

I have found in my consulting work, that for whatever reason, people want to over-complicate things. One of the reasons we fear change is because we know we are likely to create complex solutions. We fail to break solutions down into smaller steps that are more manageable. We may also set unrealistic expectations of what can be accomplished. We have all been burned by change initiatives that grew out of control, shifted scope more times than we could count, and failed to achieve anything like the expected outcomes we had hoped for.

It's time for you to look at change differently. Let's make it simple.

My goal is to give you an uncomplicated process you can use in your company, no matter how big (or how small). We will start with simple concepts. We will touch on some issues to watch out for, and focus on what you can do to start implementing these processes in your company immediately.

When people make "apples to apples" comparisons, they are looking at the products or services from different competitors, hoping to find one that will provide the best solution for their particular needs. As I have said before, if all offerings appear equal, then price is the aspect that will drive the purchase decision.

### Master the Five Tasks of the Golden Apple

We are looking to create a way to distinguish you from your competition so that price is less of a factor. We want to make your company a Golden Apple that stands apart from what the other 90 percent of your industry is doing.

Golden Apples are usually recognized as industry leaders in their own right. Price is less of a factor because Golden Apple companies respond to a need that no one else can fill. As a result, their products or services command a premium price. They get the best clients because they are recognized as different, innovative, visionary, and focused, not to mention, delivering an excellent return on investment. Golden Apples stand out from their competition and claim a highly desirable position in the marketplace.

To become a Golden Apple company, you need to focus on five tasks related to building your brand from the inside out. The labels I have given the *Five Tasks of the Golden Apple* are as follows:

- Direction,
- Path,
- People,
- Process, and
- Measures.

**Direction** deals with results—the outcomes you wish to create. This is the visionary side of business. It asks you to imagine what your company can become. Visionary positioning is important to provide the direction necessary to align resources to a common goal. Chapter 4 takes you deep into the subject of direction.

**Path** is the road you will take to get to your destination. The path has landmarks: goals you need to achieve, obstacles you need to overcome, and questions you need to answer that will reinforce your direction. Creating the right path for your business will probably involve change. As I said before, change is likely to create fear. In Chapter 5, I provide tools to help you define your path, as well as, share some ideas that will help you more effectively manage change in your organization.

**People** are the primary drivers for your business. People fall into two groups; internal and external. Internal people are those directly connected to your organization. External people are your customers, vendors, and prospects. The first group is the engine for your business; the latter provides the fuel to make it successful. In Chapter 6, you will learn how to align internal staff and receive feedback from external customers and prospects in a way that puts fuel in the engine and powers you down your path.

**Process** is an important part of any business. Process provides you the opportunity to meet customer needs with consistency. Flexible but rigorously maintained and monitored processes make it easier to train staff, manage costs, and maintain quality. While processes are about standardization there is a fine line here. Too much process can shut down innovation if people are not given the appropriate latitude to search for better ways to do things. In Chapter 7, I delve into techniques to effectively manage your business processes while encouraging innovation.

**KNOW THIS**

### People Affect Every Aspect
*Although "People" is its own task among the Five Tasks of the Golden Apple, it directly impacts all the other tasks. You cannot affect direction, path, process, or measures without directly impacting people—and vice versa.*

**Measures** follow the other four tasks that come together to produce Golden Apple companies. Measures let you know to what extent you are doing the right things. Leading indicators and lagging indicators can tell you a lot about how successful you are going to be at reaching your goals. In Chapter 8, I take up the topic of business metrics.

### Simplify!
*Whenever possible simplify the process. Assess the reason for the complexity; define why it is important. Determine costs related to your current practice in terms of time, money, and talent. Ask if there is a better way and if the answer is yes, embrace it. Follow up and monitor the results.*

**DO THIS**

If you are successful at addressing all five tasks, you can achieve the stature of the Golden Apples. But first you must commit to doing the work. You know how people sometimes just want to try something out to see if it's going to work? They adopt a new behavior for a little while and if it gets too difficult, or fails to produce results as fast as they would like, or is met with resistance from others, they take the easy way out and quit.

Reading this book represents a relatively low commitment. If you purchased the workbook to go with it then you have invested a little more into your success. But you still need to commit to doing this work if you are going to take your company to Golden Apple status.

### What Makes a "Golden Apple"?
*The five chapters in Part II present the five tasks business leaders must undertake to take their companies to Golden Apple stature—those aspects of business that together, once mastered, result in effective differentiation.*

**DO THIS**

## What Happens When a Company Becomes a Golden Apple?

What happens when you take control of your organization's direction, path, people, process, and measures? What can you achieve once you look inward, clearly define what your differences are, then communicate that message outward, so people truly get it? You will experience increased profits, lower costs, greater stability, and improved ability to recruit employees. Let's look closer at each.

### Increased Profits

What is the number one problem with commoditization? It drives the price of a product or service down because people know they can get the same thing from Company A or Company B. The cheapest product is perceived to be just as good as the more expensive offering. If you can clearly differentiate who you are, what you do, and how your product or service is going to help the consumer, it is automatically going to allow you to charge more because there is a differentiator. The consumer's decision is no longer based on price alone, it's based on whatever you have been able to incorporate, that until now, has not been available. Instantly you have the opportunity to make more money on it. Take Best Buy and computers. You'll find a bunch of desktops or laptops that with the exception of a few cosmetic changes are virtually identical. They are the Cavaliers or Escorts of the world. There might be bells and whistles built in that change the cost of the product. Toshiba and Sony? Loyalty to those brands will drive your decision, and if you aren't loyal to either brand, it comes down to "This one costs $700 and this one's $800 for basically the same features."

**KNOW THIS**

### Golden Apples Stand Out
*Golden Apples manage all five tasks exceptionally well, and so experience growth, profitability, and recognition.*

That is something the computer industry is known for. It's hard to make apples to apples comparisons because they bundle different features. One might have more RAM. One might have a faster processor, or more hard drive space, or a better graphics card. Computer companies have gotten very good at slightly changing the products so you cannot do a true comparison. For example, if you go through and look at all the brands of laptops in a Best Buy, your middle to high-end laptop will cost $700 up to maybe $1500, yet Apple laptops start at $1100. That is one of the wider spreads you will ever see, and that's the magic of differentiation. From a functionality standpoint, most computer users can accomplish most tasks on either platform, but Apple has a reputation for using higher-end products in manufacturing. A better case, screen, and so on, means durability; that is a differentiator.

---

**Leave a Legacy**

*Apple's differentiation has been based almost completely on the innovative genius of Steve Jobs. What will happen to the company when Jobs no longer serves in that role? Great business leaders consider their legacy. Time will reveal what consideration Jobs has given to this important aspect.*

**KNOW THIS**

---

Another example is gourmet chocolates and coffees. You see huge price differences. Starbucks coffee—is it really that much better than others? McDonalds has really capitalized on the recent recession by going after Starbucks. They've modified their coffee to more of a barista-type product, changed the packaging and presentation, to make it compete with Starbucks. However, on Starbucks' side, to some extent, it's the flavor of their coffee, but it's really more the branding. You can find a similar or better-quality product at a locally-owned coffee shop, but the culture you'll find at Starbucks is what they play to. If you like Starbucks you are in a hip niche, you are a trendy person. The way they teach people a special language about the drinks—the Venti and the Grande, the Macchiato—it creates a culture where some people are insiders, because they can rattle off these strange names for the drink orders. It creates a feeling of belonging by being an insider.

**KNOW THIS**

### Dunkin' Donuts
*Dunkin Donuts won with their coffee. They now supply McDonalds' with their brand.*

What McDonalds' did was to take a $4 cup of coffee and sell it for $1.50, which in this economy anyone can afford. The result; they are whipping Starbucks, which lost its way, by focusing on growth so much that they were not prepared when the recession hit their customers. Starbucks became overconfident and saturated the marketplace, so how can you support that model when there are three Starbucks within three blocks?

### Lower Costs

True differentiation moves a business toward lower costs by the law of volume. When your company stands out from the pack, you are able to increase the volume you can handle. Many expenses in an organization reach a certain threshold where the actual cost of producing that product stays very close to the same. The cost of the infrastructure to run a business hits a line where it evens out as the company sells more. Everything above that becomes profit.

Plus, you have a better opportunity to negotiate discount pricing from your vendors when you are buying in volume. Most companies (at least from a product standpoint) will agree to volume pricing for a good customer.

Depending on your structure and philosophy, and the values of your organization, you might pass those cost savings through to the customer. Even Apple has been working to lower the price points of their products. Everyone was expecting the iPad to list for $1100 but they came in at a price point of $500. Now, I challenge anyone to get it at $500 with all the little accessories you need to get it to work. Your $500 iPad turns into an $800 iPad, and somehow you perceive that as customizing rather than being nickled and dimed.

There are ways to maximize the profitability of an organization. You have to look at the realities of the marketplace you are in. If there are not a lot of competitors, it allows you to move that price point further back and forth on a scale. If you are up against a lot of competition, you have to be more price-conscious. You have to look at a lot of different variables.

Your decision whether you pass cost advantages along in lower prices is driven by company culture. You can either take profits for yourself, or if you are very customer-centric, you can decide to reward loyal customers by showing them that you do not eat up the profits but turn around and put some of that into cost savings for customers.

### Company Culture is Dramatic in its Impact

Culture can be hard to see. Sometimes it looks like décor. The underlying theme of this entire book is how company culture affects every aspect of your business. Until you explore your culture—how you go about defining who you are as a company, how your product will interact with your customers, how *you* will interact with your customers—you cannot expect to become a Golden Apple. Company culture drives differentiation in virtually every business. Where there is a lack of company culture, commoditization begins. People have nothing to hang onto besides the product or service. And if it's the same or similar to a competitor, it comes down to "which one is going to cost me less?"

Culture exists whether you consciously create it or not. Just as every buying decision is an emotional one, and even indifference is an emotion, every organization has a culture. That culture is primarily driven by the leaders of the organization. Whether or not you focus on your culture, you will have one. Is it going to be one that allows you to sustain and build your business? Or have you been successful in spite of a lackluster culture? If so, when it catches up with you, it's going to be a painful process because now you have to reinvent yourself and figure out how you get from Point A to Point B. You can leave it to chance or take control.

American Girl has done a phenomenal job of taking a $5 doll and turning it into a $150 doll, and then making sure every accessory you add is $20 or $30. My daughter has one. Her grandmother got it for her. We went to the American Girl Place Chicago store on Michigan Avenue. You would never know there was a recession going on. It was wall-to-wall people and they were all buying products. In my world, what's wrong with a $5 doll? Yet they have created a culture around the product and really changed it. I can find similar dolls in style and quality, but they don't come with the whole culture around the doll that American Girl Company delivers.

**KNOW THIS**

### Create "Raving Fans"
*Ken Blanchard and Sheldon Bowles wrote* Raving Fans: A Revolutionary Approach To Customer Service. *Their fundamental insight is that businesses don't just need "satisfied" customers who will do business with you only until a better competitor comes along, but "raving fans"— people who advocate for your products or services in the marketplace. Think of a company that has "raving fans." Depending on your interests, you might call to mind a sports team, a computer company, a doll manufacturer, or something entirely different. Whatever company came to mind—what makes it different? How does it earn its "raving fans"?*

Build-A-Bear is another example of a product with an experience that goes with it. This goes back to what we discussed earlier, that every purchase is an emotional purchase , and that there are only two emotions people deal with through their purchases, pleasure and pain. You are either trying to get away from pain or get more pleasure. What American Girl and Build-A-Bear have done is embrace that concept. Build-A-Bear is an escape experience that is pleasurable and ends with a product. There is not too much about pain I can relate to these products. You look at the marketing success of these companies and you see company culture at work.

These companies have achieved true differentiation, and the lower cost structure that comes with it goes straight to their bottom lines.

### Greater Stability

Greater stability comes from differentiation because in the process of differentiating your product or service, you gain a clearer understanding of your vision, your culture and what makes you different. Your sales go up, your costs maintain or go down, and that offers stability. Now you are able to grow intelligently.

Growing intelligently leads to greater stability. When you are growing intelligently, you are hiring the right number of people at the right time. You are able to train them sufficiently rather than throw them in to learn by trial or error. They are more a part of the company, they understand the culture better and they feel more integrated with that culture.

**KNOW THIS**

**Businessmen or Firemen?**
*Are your leaders' businessmen or firemen? Proactive or reactive? This has an impact on stability. Master the tasks of the Golden Apple to move from firefighting to leading.*

The business that fails to achieve stability through differentiation suffers the consequences. Its product becomes commoditized, which means companies with the power to undercut pricing will do so, resulting in a greater perception of competition even if the field of vendors remains the same. If you find yourself in that pitfall, you're forced to make decisions. Faced with declining sales, you have to cut back. And where do you usually cut back? All the training and development goes out the window. And yet you expect your staff to be more creative and more productive than they were in the past. You are asking them to figure it out without training, and that leads to the downward tumble. Now you have to cut deeper so you start looking at laying people off. You might restructure the company or let certain people go. Those lay-offs incite more panic because the people who were not laid off are questioning the viability of the company. Now they start to think, "I'm doing my work plus John Doe's work, my workload's doubled, and no one's telling me how to prioritize." Increasing stress causes productivity to drop further, and it's a slippery slope that compounds all the problems.

### Improved Recruitment

When you stand out from the competition, when you are perceived as an employer of choice, you do not have to search for talent. Talent comes to you. Much like any of the cool products we have been talking about, the law of supply and demand kicks in. There are more people who want to work for you. You can be choosier with the type of people you hire. From a company standpoint, you will now get better people at a lower cost. People want to work for a company where they are going to be valued, where they are going to have some level of engagement, where they feel that the work they do is important. If the current job they have does not provide that, they may stick it out because jobs are hard to find in a down economy, but that's hurting you as an employer company even more. Those employees are probably not fully engaged—they are not doing the best job possible. They will not leave, but do just what they need to do to make sure they continue collecting that paycheck.

An example of a company that experienced improved recruitment as the result of business strategy can be drawn from Land's End. When they first relocated from the Chicago area to rural Wisconsin back in the 1970s and 1980s, the economy was in recession. The move helped them cut costs by making them the employer of choice. They were in a region where the dominant industry was agriculture. Access to better jobs was limited—the nearest city, of any size, is 45 miles away. Lands' End gave people the opportunity to do something other than milk cows and bale hay.

Why did Lands' End succeed with this strategy?

The leaders were visionary and effective. They conveyed that they really cared for their employees with actions like providing an excellent work environment (they were one of the first to offer an on-site exercise facility for employees), a great benefit package, and work that was attractive compared to other jobs available in the area. The company was in an expansion mode, in spite of the recession, and that in itself was attractive—everybody wants to play for a winning team.

The location decision gave Lands' End a point of differentiation that they played up in their culture and their brand. They spun it in a positive way, embraced the rural culture and made it an advertising message. As the Lands' End example shows, differentiation can lead to improved recruitment, which means you attract higher-quality people at reasonable cost. You become the employer of choice.

## Ready to Commit to the Five Tasks of the Golden Apple?

I've introduced you to the five tasks that, when given your attention, will make your brand a Golden Apple from the inside out—Direction, Path, People, Process, and Measures. Notice I didn't say "when completed" because these tasks are never really "done." You will need to keep applying your attention to the five tasks to maintain your competitive edge as a Golden Apple.

I've given you a taste of the success factors that will come your way once you become that Golden Apple—increased profits, lower costs, greater stability, and easier recruiting of the best talent. Sounds good, right?

The benefits of being that Golden Apple that stands out among competitors and commands a premium price will keep you motivated. You should feel no urge to quit along the way if you follow the steps as I lay them out for you in the upcoming chapters. Do your research, put in the time, and complete the tasks. Your strategic plan for differentiation will fall into place.

Commitment is the starting point. When the work gets difficult, you will press on, and you won't give up. You may come upon new information as you go along that requires you to take a step back, re-evaluate a strategy, and chart a new course. Then it will be important to stick to your new path.

Your commitment starts here. Your first step: Read on.

# PART 2

## The Five Tasks of the Golden Apple

# The First Task of the Golden Apple: Direction

The first task of a Golden Apple company is to find its Direction. Determining direction is all about your vision of what your company can become. Without direction, it's impossible to align resources to achieve a common goal.

While most companies understand there is a value to developing statements of vision, mission, and values, too often their approach is not tied to action. How do you define your direction in a way that is not only inspirational and meaningful to your leaders, board, and staff, but also deliverable?

> **Tell Stories!**
> *Rarely do you hear about telling a story when it comes to planning. In fact, it was hard to find many good examples doing research for this book. The truth is--the story is an important part of the business plan. It helps create consistency in the message and provides another relevant point of communication to engage your staff in the direction you wish to go.*
>
> **KNOW THIS**

What you need is a compelling story that brings your direction to life. The compelling story provides a way for the senior leadership to grasp the vision, mission, and values, and how they add up to an actionable direction for the company. It explains what this really means for us and why it is important. It's part of human nature— we are accustomed to storytelling as part of our learning process. We have been learning this way for centuries. Story telling is how we pass along our personal values and beliefs. The compelling story becomes the unifying feature that pulls the vision, mission, and values together into one cohesive idea that shows where this company is going.

In this chapter we will work on finding the right direction for your company by examining your mission, vision, and values, then translating that into a compelling story. We will consider your past, present, and future to determine what elements need to be part of that compelling story. Finally, I'll show you the impact your leaders have on your ability to move efficiently in your chosen direction.

## Your Vision, Mission and Values, Point to Your Direction

When I explain vision, mission, and values to my clients, I tell them it's like picking a travel destination. Let's pretend that you are in New York City and trying to get to Los Angeles. You might know Los Angeles is in a westerly direction, but without some sort of roadmap to get you there, you could waste a lot of resources and time. *Vision* is the ability to see that future point clearly, to see what you want to become.

If *vision* is the destination, then *mission* is the highway you choose to get there. Different highways will get you from New York to Los Angeles. You consider the possible routes and you choose one. Take that New York to Los Angeles trip—if your mission is to enjoy the beautiful country in between, you might choose a route that winds through a number of our national parks. If your mission is to arrive as quickly as possible, then you'll choose a more direct route and skip the scenery. Mission guides strategic decisions about how you reach your destination.

Now we get to your *values*. Picture a multi-lane highway, three or four lanes wide. Values are the lines that keep you out of the ditch. Your values should give you room to move around on the highway so you can dodge obstacles as they come. But you know if you go outside of your values, you are headed for a wreck.

> **What Sets You Apart?**
> This book will break the search for the answer to that
> question into components related to product, culture,
> marketing, and leadership. You will learn basic, consistent
> steps that help you apply these components in your search
> for the "thing" that differentiates your company. You will learn
> how to look at factors like marketing in a new way, to find
> and communicate the one clear message that gets people to
> understand what makes you different from the rest.

KNOW THIS

That is the analogy I use when I am describing vision, mission, and values because it illustrates why each is so important. Let's look closer at each of these aspects of your company's direction, beginning with your vision.

Talk about your vision, mission, and values as often as possible. Relate experiences, situations, and outcomes to each of these areas. In other words, tell stories that illustrate how your company walks its talk, and the good things that happen as a result.

*Building Vision*

Coming up in this chapter you will find an exercise in which I ask you to imagine your business in the future without obstacles. The point is to develop your vision of what you want to become. The exercise challenges you to think about your company's future in detail in terms of the financial picture, your operational picture, your staffing, your market, your innovation, your leadership.

> **Think Without Limits**
> Why do I suggest you remove obstacles from your thinking
> about Vision? By taking away the obstacles, you are able
> to focus on what you want to create or become. Obstacles
> have a funny way of limiting thinking and throw us back
> into problem-solving mode, which can cause us to lose
> focus. There are plenty of opportunities later in the process
> to address business challenges and feed your need to fix
> things. We will get to those later.

KNOW THIS

In the next chapter we will examine the path that connects your business today with your business as you envision it in the future. We will identify strengths, weaknesses, opportunities, and threats, to find the gaps and obstacles you face and your strategy to move beyond them.

But before we go there, let's try to get that vision you have down to a clear, passionate, concise, and condensed vision statement.

The vision helps your staff align their actions. It invokes a level of passion. It shows how what you are doing is significant.

You might have participated in a process of drafting a vision statement in the past. Maybe it involved a couple hours of discussion about where you want to go. In some companies, that's fine. They have a pretty clear understanding of what they want to become and the session is really just about aligning those thoughts. In other companies, especially those that have never done much planning, the vision statement needs to be dealt with in more depth. It may not be something you can hammer out in a couple of hours.

This is not about looking for those inspiring words you can slap on a plaque and mount on a wall and then walk past without a thought. I am less concerned about using the 25-cent words and more concerned about the effect the vision statement has on the organization, its leaders and its people.

I suggest you invest enough time to make sure that your vision statement really conveys something to you about what you want to become, and can be said in a couple of sentences, so everyone gets it and can remember it.

**KNOW THIS**

### *A Vision is More than Words*

*Vision is more than just some great-sounding words. Your goal in drafting a vision statement is to come up with one or two concise motivational sentences. Stick to the present tense. A great vision statement can be condensed to just a few words, like newspaper publisher William Randolph Hearst's dictum, "Get it first and get it right."*

A vision statement that is too lengthy is trying to take on too much. Be careful that your Vision reflects the views of the leadership and culture. Executives have a key role here. Avoid striving for consensus. It is often joked that a camel is a horse designed by a committee. Senior leadership drives Vision, Mission, and Values, not the committee.

You are not willing to take the risk to say, "We will do this and only this, even if it means we have to give up other things. We are focusing all our efforts on becoming this one thing." Failing to focus leads to dilution to a point where there is no differentiation. A vision statement that is too broad is just going to create confusion. This process's purpose is to drill down to your most closely-held beliefs, then articulate them in a concise and motivational way. The vision statement should be something everyone in the company can remember.

### Seek Feedback

*When working on your Vision, Mission, and Values, seek feedback from other members of your leadership team. The point here is not to build consensus, but an understanding of what they believe your Vision is. It is a good test for alignment as you move forward in the planning process.*

**DO THIS**

When you are building your team to work on the vision statement, who you bring into the room matters. Do not just invite the people you are comfortable with. You want to generate a spirited discussion that pulls people out of their comfort zones. To really find out what your vision is, you have to challenge those things you hold near and dear. Sometimes those factors are actually weaknesses that are holding you back. Your vision team must include people who will challenge those thoughts and ideas, bringing those weaknesses to light. Having the right mix of people working on the vision matters.

The other factor is having the right number of people. It is possible to have too few and not get enough viewpoints. It is also

**DO THIS**

> ## Mix Up the Party!
> *As you begin the planning process, consider the people you will invite to participate. Who will challenge beliefs in a way that will create a better outcome? Who will be able to dig into the details and question ideas? Who is connected to the people and desires harmony in a group environment? A mixture of these types is necessary to strengthen your plan.*

possible to have too many. The ideal planning group I look for is somewhere around six people. If you have too many different viewpoints, opinions, and agendas, it gets difficult to manage. I am not concerned about odd or even numbers—it's not like voting. You need to build a consensus.

I have had groups working on vision with 20 or more people in a room. Those groups were very difficult. Everyone has a different idea what direction the vision process should take. In a large group, you spend too much of your time arguing about where the process is going to go, and not enough time getting to work. I have worked with smaller groups where they clicked so well, we moved through the process very quickly, with very positive results. It comes down to how clearly the people in the group understand each other and the ultimate outcome they are trying to create. The group's task is to pull out what is important to an organization, and focus on how to apply it.

When you are done with this process, whether it takes hours or days, you should have your vision down to no more than two sentences that are clear and concise, yet broad enough to reach a large audience and not pigeon-hole you too much. It's a bit of a contradiction, the search for that sweet spot. The vision statement should resonate with the leadership team and the people throughout the organization. It should capture what drives the passion—what makes a person want to go to work here, versus anywhere else, any given day.

➡️

There is a story about Walt Disney and how he came by his vision for Disneyland. He took his family to visit an amusement park.
Back in mid 20th-century America, amusement parks were pretty
seedy places, if you looked below the glamorous surface impres-
sion. They had more in common with carnivals and circuses than
the theme parks of today. Walt was disappointed at all the chipped
paint and broken machinery he encountered. In his mind, he could
see an amusement park where young and old alike could enjoy the
excitement and razzle-dazzle without the dirt and disappointment.
It was not a positive family experience, but it did give Walt a vision
of what amusement parks could be. His vision boiled down to, "No
chipped paint. All the rides work."

Here are a few more examples that pass my test: they are concise, motivating, and easily remembered.

- Abbott Laboratories: "Abbott's vision is to be the world's
  premier health care company. Simply put, we want to be
  the best - the best employer, the best health care supplier,
  the best business partner, the best investment and the best
  neighbor."
- Apple Computer: "Start a revolution in the way the average
  person processes information."
- Avon beauty products: "Be the company that best understands and satisfies the product, service and self-fulfillment
  needs of women—globally."
- Caterpillar: "Be the global leader in customer value."
- Dish Network: "To provide quality products through a world
  class sales organization to every home in America."
- Disney: "To make people happy."
- Federal Express: "Truly reliable mail service."
- Google: "Google's mission is to organize the world's infor-
  mation and make it universally accessible and useful."
- Hewlett Packard: "To view change in the market as an
  opportunity to grow; to use our profits and our ability to

develop and produce innovative products, services and solutions that satisfy emerging customer needs."

- Kraft Foods: "Help people around the world eat and live better."
- Nordstrom's: "Create an experience with our stores."
- And then there is my own company's vision statement! In-Vision Business Development: "To help people discover their unique path to success."

Finding and stating your vision is just one part of the task of the Golden Apple Company that I call Direction. It is one clear differentiator that can truly move you forward. But it only works if it ties into the culture of the company. What's your mission? What are your values? That's your next focus. Going back to the travel analogy I used at the start of this chapter, the vision gives you the purpose of the trip. The mission is what gives you a direction to go in.

## Mission

The words "vision" and "mission" tend to mean different things to different people. To me, "Mission" is more finite. A mission statement describes goals that can be accomplished in three to five years.

The mission tends to be a high-level statement, for example, "We will create an international side to our company by 20XX." A mission will break down into specific strategies, supported by operational steps you have to accomplish to get there. When I look at strategies, I apply the rule of "three to five." Most people can retain and remember three to five concepts. You may have more strategies than that, but I will ask you to focus on the top three to five strategies that support your mission. And I will ask you to keep your framework at no more than a two- or three-year window.

The world is going to change. Before the technological advances of the last decade or two, you did not have to worry about what went on outside your own locale. Now, you have to worry about the guy on the other side of the world as much as the guy across the street. Strategies have to be broader. You cannot get too specific beyond a two-year window, because there is just too much 'what-if' coming into play.

You have to be nimble, be able to change your strategy to respond. Your mission statement should be high-level enough that the pace of change is not going to make it obsolete in six months or a year. Rather, it should apply to the three- to five-year horizon.

Here are a few examples of Mission statements that fit my definition, that is, high-level statements that describe goals to be accomplished in a set timeframe.

- Achieve total annual revenue of $500 million by 20XX
- Own 20 percent market share in IT consulting by Q4, 20XX
- Have over 80 percent of our new business through referrals by the end of 20XX

In the next chapter, I will fold this concept of "mission" into the Path—the second task of every Golden Apple company.

*Values*

Returning to our travel analogy, vision gives you purpose for the trip; mission gives you a direction to go in to achieve that purpose; values keep you from veering off that route. Values are what enable people in the company to innovate and to make decisions on their own, and still stay aligned with the overall mission and vision of that company.

A sociologist would define "values" as the ideals, customs, and so on that the people of a group hold in high regard. That's what I'm talking about here—the shared ideals that give a group common ground and a shared sense of what is right, and worth working for. Build your corporate culture around values—the words you live by.

In my consulting I take people through an exercise in which I ask them to write down all the values they believe exist within their organization. I will then ask them to prioritize that list. What are your top three to five values? You could try this right now.

Look at the list. Maybe you came up with the list of 20 words. In most cases, some will be very similar. Start grouping things together. Your list will get shorter.

I find a lot of the words used to describe specific values are actually just different ways of saying the same thing. For example, there are a lot of traits that roll up to integrity—If you put honesty and commitment on your list, you can decide to group those under the value of integrity, and move on.

It is important to identify those traits you can roll up into a single word because you need to get the list down to no more than five points. If you cannot count it on one hand, it is going to be very difficult for people to remember. You really have to work to uncover which are the most important values in your company's culture.

Prioritize the list again. Keep working it until you have found the top three to five values that are fundamentally your rules of engagement for business. They state how you are going to operate and what you agree that you are not going to do.

**DO THIS**

### List, then Narrow Down
*Make a list of values that are meaningful to your organization. For your first pass, do not limit the length of the list—include as many values on the list as you need to. Once your list is formed, narrow it down to no more than five separate values. (Again you will see my faith in the rule of "three to five.") Take the time to define what those values mean to your leadership and staff.*

If somebody in your organization takes an action outside of those values, you will be breaking trust with your clients and with your coworkers. You are really not living the purpose for which your company exists. If you are going to claim integrity as a value, you had better understand what you mean by that word, and make sure that your customers know too. That will be the first thing you get called out on if you do not live up to that particular value. The same goes for honesty, transparency, and so on.

Here are some values my company lives by:

- Boundless thinking: We will continue to look for possibilities not only for our clients, but ourselves. We will find opportunities and continue to ask "What if" or "How can we..."
- Servant Approach: Our clients and their success are the reasons we exist. We are committed to helping them realize their goals. Through this, we will realize ours.
- Trust: It is absolutely critical that we obtain the trust of our clients, our colleagues, and the communities in which we serve. This trust allows us to open up new possibilities throughout all areas of our business and our lives.
- Empowerment: Our ultimate goal is getting the right people doing the right things and being driven by a deeper purpose and commitment. We will help leaders uncover the strengths and passion in their people and the techniques to allow them to use it.

## The Compelling Story

Once you are crystal-clear on your company's vision, mission, and values, it is time to turn them into a compelling story.

What is the story that explains where you have come from, where you are, what you want to become, and how you are going to achieve that? What in that story conveys your passion for your business? What makes it feel important?

We all relate to a good story. Take movies, or the parables in the Bible, or the human-interest stories in the news media. They are all built around the human instinct for stories. If you can create a story that people want to associate with, it aligns their passion with your direction. They now get a picture of where you are going and what you are doing and why they are important and why they need to be there and be part of it.

The compelling story gets deeper into the "why." Why is this our vision of what we will do? Why have we chosen one mission over another? Why are certain values so important they make it onto our short list?

**KNOW THIS**

### *Compelling Stories Communicate Passion*

*A compelling story captures what your company is passionate about. A compelling story helps pass that message down through the organization. It's also a great tool for marketing.*

The compelling story is designed to create greater clarity for the staff and the customers as to what the company is all about. It makes it memorable through example.

Consider the following examples of compelling stories:

### *Disney: "Unparalleled Entertainment Experiences"*

Since its founding in 1923, the Walt Disney Company and its affiliated companies have remained faithful to their commitment to produce unparalleled entertainment experiences based on the rich legacy of quality creative content and exceptional storytelling. The Walt Disney Company, together with its subsidiaries and affiliates, is a leading diversified international family entertainment and media enterprise with four business segments: media networks, parks and resorts, studio entertainment and consumer products.

### *3M: "Milestones"*

3M was founded in 1902 in the Lake Superior town of Two Harbors, Minnesota. Five businessmen set out to mine a mineral deposit for grinding-wheel abrasives. But the deposits proved to be of little value, and the new Minnesota Mining and Manufacturing Company quickly moved to nearby Duluth in 1905 to focus on sandpaper products.

Years of struggle ensued until the company could master quality production and supply chain. New investors were attracted to 3M, such as Lucius Ordway, who moved the company to St. Paul in 1910. Early technical and marketing innovations began to produce successes and, in 1916, the company paid its first dividend of six cents a share.

The world's first waterproof sandpaper, which reduced airborne dusts during automotive manufacturing, was developed in the early 1920s.

A second major milestone occurred in 1925 when Richard G. Drew, a young lab assistant, invented masking tape—an innovative step toward diversification and the first of many Scotch brand pressure-sensitive tapes.

In the following years technical progress resulted in Scotch® Cellophane Tape for box sealing and soon hundreds of practical uses were discovered.

In the early 1940s, 3M was diverted into defense materials for World War II, which was followed by new ventures, such as Scotchlite™ Reflective Sheeting for highway markings, magnetic sound recording tape, filament adhesive tape, and the start of 3M's involvement in the graphic arts with offset printing plates.

In the 1950s, 3M introduced the Thermo-Fax™ copying process, Scotchgard™ Fabric Protector, videotape, Scotch-Brite® Cleaning Pads and several new electro-mechanical products.

Dry-silver microfilm was introduced in the 1960s, along with photographic products, carbonless papers, overhead projection systems, and a rapidly growing health care business of medical and dental products.

Markets further expanded in the 1970s and 1980s into pharmaceuticals, radiology and energy control.

In 1980, 3M introduced Post-it® Notes, which created a whole new category in the marketplace and changed people's communication and organization behavior forever.

In the 1990s sales reached the $15 billion mark. 3M continued to develop an array of innovative products, including immune response modifier pharmaceuticals; brightness enhancement films for electronic displays; and flexible circuits used in inkjet printers, cell phones and other electronic devices.

In 2004, sales topped $20 billion for the first time with innovative new products contributing significantly to growth. Recent innovations include Post-it® Super Sticky Notes, Scotch® Transparent Duct Tape, optical films for LCD televisions, and a new family of Scotch-Brite® cleaning products that give consumers the right scrubbing power for a host of cleaning jobs.

### Nordstrom's: "Leave It Better than We Found It"

We have always followed a simple philosophy when it comes to running our business: Leave it better than you found it. This also describes Nordstrom's commitment to social responsibility. Since our early days, we have focused on doing the right thing for our employees and our customers. We continue to make every effort to be an ethical company where people want to work and shop. We are working to leave it better than we found it.

Whether you opt for a timeline approach like 3M (which can get lengthy for a company that has passed the century mark) or a concise story like Disney's or Nordstrom's, the compelling story becomes a tool for communicating about your business.

The compelling story will give your advertising agency or marketing company direction. It tells them, "We are the experts on who we are. You are the experts on getting this message out to the public." All too often, I have seen companies (especially smaller organizations) throw full control over their brand and their identity to a company they have just hired. That company does not have the same degree of understanding that the people in the organization have about where the company is going. What is scary is the high dollar investment you make in any form of advertising. If you are allowing somebody else to control your story and it does not align with who you really are, you are setting yourself for failure.

The compelling story is very useful in orienting new hires. Whenever you are bringing in an outside consultant and you want to get them up to speed on your business, that compelling story, combined with the work on vision, mission, and values, gives them a clearly articulated sense of your company's purpose.

Most businesses are challenged with differentiating themselves because they have not clearly identified their purpose. What is their reason for existence? The clearer that purpose, the greater the likelihood of success for that business, assuming the purpose has market value.

---

### The Purpose of "Purpose"

*"Purpose" is more about what problems you solve than what you do. What value does the purpose bring to customers, employees, investors, and the world at large?*

KNOW THIS

---

When you can define your purpose clearly, other people can attach themselves to it. Your employees, your customers—they all understand on an emotional level what value the purpose brings to them. What is that deep-seated emotion that really causes you to buy into something? Why do people buy organic food instead of conventional products? The answer is deeply emotional. It may have to do with personal health, or supporting small local businesses, or a feeling of doing the right thing in the world, or positively affecting the environment. It goes back to people wanting to have purpose and significance. They need to know why doing business with you is going to align with their own values, their own search for meaning.

Your compelling story in its early stages might be adjusted as strategic planning progresses. In fact, the whole suite of compo-

---

### The Compelling Story Conveys Company Culture

*Your compelling story conveys the essence of your company's culture. It communicates the core ideas and beliefs your leaders, staff, and customers will experience. It shows how you put the values you have defined into action. It lays the groundwork for increased staff retention, capacity for innovation and growth, and good communication throughout the organization. Above all, it sets your direction as an organization focused on delivering customer satisfaction.*

KNOW THIS

nents that make up the task of Direction—vision, mission, values, a compelling story—are interdependent. You cannot finalize any one component without taking the others into account. When you are through with the process, first roughing together some wording for each, and then testing and discussing, and boiling those words in your team process, you will have arrived at a deep understanding of your company. You will have something customers and employees can form a deep personal bond to.

## Your Company: The History Lesson

If thinking about your mission, vision, values, and compelling story leaves you feeling this is all too intangible, let me bring you back to a solid starting point—your company's history.

What put you where you are at today? Was it that you were first in your industry? Did you have lower cost, or unique technology, or the best reputation, or greater visibility because of your advertising?

Before there were automobiles, there were horse carriages. Somebody had to decide to try putting an engine on that carriage. At first there were individual carriage workers basically building automobiles by hand. Then Henry Ford figured out a way to mass-produce an identical vehicle over and over again, which significantly dropped the cost, and made it available to a mass market. Ford got the lead on mass production and became the industry leader.

"First in the industry" can be important, if you stay innovative and keep ahead of the game. This is where a lot of people lose ground because they come into the industry, or they create the industry, and then others follow their lead, learn how to do it better, and beat them or swallow them up. "First" is a hard position to maintain.

What you may discover by looking at your history lesson is that what got you started is not going to carry you forward. You might also learn where opportunities exist that you can expand or grow into.

A good place to focus your attention, as you ask where you came from, is to consider what prompted people to buy from you. That gets at the customer's perspective on your company as opposed to your own internal perspective. If you look at certain product-driven companies, you will find there was something about what they did and how they did it that connected with a certain group of customers. Apple hit a core niche. Microsoft hit a different niche. That history has become part of their DNA, and influences where these companies are today and where they will go in the future.

The takeaway from this part of the history lesson could be that what got you started is still working for you, or you may find that you have ridden that horse as far is it will go, and you will need to turn to innovation for your company to thrive in the future.

### Innovation Based on Experience

The innovation that carries you forward may spring from seeing your company as a culture, an experience. Let me give you a couple of examples. The original environment these companies came from influenced what their culture is like, and that connects to their product and what it is going to do for you.

An example of a company that innovated to sustain and grow its early market success is Disney. In the beginning, Disney was a movie studio making animated features. Those animated features grew into a vision that Walt Disney had of bringing an experience to life and allowing people to be absorbed in it. It only took an encounter with a dirty, run-down amusement park for him to realize this was a huge opportunity.

Disney turned that realization into a vision to create an environment where families could go interact with the characters he had created, in a place that was safe and fun for all ages. Out of that he created Disneyland in Anaheim, California. Disneyland almost failed, but they fixed bugs and grew, and that led to Disney World and more theme parks and now, it's a global brand, based on a specific culture and experience.

Another company comes to mind as an example of success that comes from celebrating a culture, an experience. That is the Green Bay Packers football franchise. You cannot take in a broadcast of a Packers game, especially when it's a home game at Lambeau Field, without hearing the announcers talk about the experience of Lambeau Field. Built in 1957, it is one of the oldest football stadiums still in use by a professional team. It's a shrine for the football fans. They will tell you that, to be a true football fan, you have to experience at least one game in Lambeau Field. Part of that experience is the story that has grown up around it and part is the actual interaction with the Lambeau environment. When it was remodeled in 2003, the Packers believed they needed to update the facility to remain financially competitive in the NFL. The massive redevelopment plan was designed to update the facilities and add more premium seating, and yet preserve the historic environment. They kept the seating bowl the same, and kept the natural grass playing field that has become known as the "frozen tundra." Lambeau Field is an essential element of the Green Bay Packers franchise, part of their recognized brand, based on a specific culture and experience just as much as the Disney theme park empire.

### History of Innovation

As you look at where you have come from, is innovations part of that story?

Corning created a new type of glass in the 1960s. At the time they could not find a use for it. Now, it has been branded as "Gorilla Glass" and its being used in flat panels for mobile phones and other devices. The glass is really thin, durable, and smooth. They did not need it in the 1960s, but they patented it, and then tucked it away for 40 years. Now, with the changes in technology, that product is the perfect solution for certain applications. It is ideal for electronics.

Start looking at the role innovation has played in creating your direction so far, and what is going to work in the future. If you are starting to see companies move in and take market share from you,

you can just worry about what they are doing, or you can worry about what is going to be the next step that keeps you two feet in front of them with something really different.

Consider the 3M Corporation. Company policy gives employees sabbaticals during which they are given a month to just create stuff. It does not matter whether it actually turns into a product or not. The company culture is about that drive to make innovation happen. There might be ten misses but there is one home run that really makes it worthwhile for 3M to continue that sabbatical policy.

The origin of the 3M Post-It Note™ comes to mind as an example of a story that gets told and retold, and it helps 3M find people that fit into their culture of innovation. A research scientist had come up with a glue that failed to stick permanently. It was useless. But someone else in 3M's research labs needed bookmarks he could put in his hymnal that would stay put through a Sunday service but not permanently damage the book. He tried the failed glue and it worked perfectly. To get 3M to take the new product idea seriously they made prototype blocks of the new sticky paper and gave them to the company's secretaries. They came up with more uses for the product than anyone had imagined.

There is a story that supports a powerful belief in 3M as a company that innovates. It makes you willing to try out new products from them. The company has a compelling story that prompts people to buy.

Google has its "20 percent time." Employees are supposed to spend 20 percent of their time exploring their own interests, and if the result migrates into a product, that is great. These are examples of innovation as part of a company's culture.

Too many companies see only the risk that comes with innovation. Most companies, whether they admit it or not, tend to be risk-adverse because they have achieved a certain level of success, and they know that there is risk that innovation is going to use up time, money, and resources. That's daunting. Fear of risk keeps companies from being truly innovative. Put innovation at the core of your

**KNOW THIS**

### *Innovation vs. Risk*
*Innovation and risk-aversion do not play well together. To innovate, you have to take risks. The job of leadership is to use planning to mitigate those risks.*

company culture, and you will have a good start on a clear answer to, "what makes you different from your competitors?"

### Business Cycles: Learning from Past Experience

To continue the history lesson, consider the business cycles that have influenced your company in the past. When your business began, what was the state of the economy? Did you get started during a period of rapid growth or one hindered by recession? What has been the trend since?

Take a look at the economic cycles you have been doing business in over the years since your company was founded. What have you learned from these cycles? Now look ahead at where you are going. Is there anything you know from the past that is relevant to your future? Or are you going to have to learn new coping mechanisms? If you began in rapid growth and all signs point to that continuing, great. But if there are warning signs that conditions are changing, do not delay in responding. The sooner you respond, the better for your business.

Long-term negative trends are the most worrisome because they are signs that changes have been taking place, but at a much slower pace, and so have been harder to detect. What is creating the negative trend may be a deep-rooted cultural issue. Most companies are not nimble enough to move when something changes, because they do not have the resources or have not thought through what the response might be.

To be more nimble, you should do some "what-if" scenarios to prepare your strategic thinking for different possibilities. Every business should do contingency planning. The more far-sighted a company can be with its people and its processes and its product,

70 ➡

the greater likelihood it is going to have something in its toolkit that will allow it to sidestep the trouble that is coming, and still be able to grow.

I am not saying this is easy. I am not going to pretend that you can immediately implement something that is going to make a difference in your business. I just think many companies do not look ahead when things are going well. They wait until something happens, which puts them in a reactive mode. Instead of managing by a good strategic plan, they have to making hard cultural shifts, pulling people out of their comfort zones, and expecting immediate improvement. That's not easy to achieve.

To wrap up the history lesson—I have asked you to think about where you got your start. What values have been part of your company culture for so long they are in your DNA? I have asked you to think about the environment in which you have operated in the past—how have business cycles affected your story? These thoughts should lead you to the lessons you can draw from your past experience. Which takes us to...

## Your Industry Today

What is going on in your industry today and how will it impact you? Some industries are growing, others not. Maybe your particular business is growing in your particular industry or maybe you are not. How does your growth pattern relate to what is going on in your marketplace?

For example, if you were making wagon wheels back in the 1800s, I am sure business was great then. But when the 1900s came along and everyone began driving around in cars, wagon wheels were pretty much obsolete. A few of the best probably kept making wagon wheels for specialty markets—people make wagon wheels today. But the average wagon wheel maker moved on when his industry changed.

My point is, even if you are the best at what you are doing, your market may be disappearing. You can either choose to specialize in a shrinking niche, so that you gain whatever market share is left, or you are going to have to look ahead at where your market is going.

Part of that looking around involves examining your competition. Where are your competitors weakest? If you would like to do the research yourself, the Internet is a wonderful tool. You will find plenty of resources online to help you discover what your competitors are doing. In many cases, you can get feedback from their clients, if they have posted anything online. There are also a number of referral sites that post customer feedback scores and comments. You can find out a lot about your competitors and what's going on in your industry right there.

**KNOW THIS**

### View "DIY" Data Impartially
*Be careful when using do-it-yourself research. Sometimes research information can be skewed by researcher bias. You must be willing to view data impartially.*

If your competitors are publicly traded companies, you can see trends in their publicly reported financial data. Are they growing or shrinking? Financially, what has been the trend? In terms of competitors' innovations, news travels rapidly. You are not going to find any of the dark, dark details in public channels, but you can still find speculation about what types of projects they are working on. If you can validate some of that information, it can give you insight into what your competitors are doing.

Take every opportunity to connect directly with customers and find out if they have done business with your competitors and what their thoughts are. Think about how new clients have come to you. They probably worked with your competitor in the past and they have switched for various reasons.

Research market trends, as well. Merely looking at competitors can put you in a "me-too" position, following their lead. Innovators anticipate market and social changes, and comprehend the needs created by those changes. Anticipating future needs gives you a direction for development.

If you would rather not rely on your own research, a number of companies specialize in competitive intelligence. You can invest money to have other companies find that information for you. You can get competitive information through purchasing survey data from a vendor making consumer recommendations, like J.D. Powers Associates and similar third-party evaluators.

It all comes back to looking at your industry, using do-it-yourself research or purchased data or a combination of both. Your job is figuring out what is changing, and whether your competitors are innovating and changing along with the industry or sticking with a reactionary position.

Once you have completed the history lesson and taken a look at what is going on in your industry, move your focus inward. What is going on inside your company? Where are you at in terms of your people, your finances, your processes, and your leadership's commitment to follow-through on new initiatives to keep you moving in your chosen direction?

## Where Are You Going?

At this point, we have talked about where you have come from. We have finished the history lesson.

You have thought about the current factors affecting your business, in terms of your ability to compete in your industry with the people, financial situation, and your process . Now, let's shift our focus to how you can create the outcome you want going forward.

### *If You Could See Your Future…*

It's time for an exercise that might change your business—even your life.

Imagine your business without any obstacles in its way. If you could create anything at all, what would you build?

Strip away all the unknowns that could prevent you from getting there. Right now, we are not going to worry about obstacles. I am just asking you to imagine, "If we could create our utopia, what would that look like? What will we be doing? How will we be doing it? Who will we be interacting with? Who will we have as employees? What will our leadership team look like?"

Sure, this creates a false sense of reality for the moment. That's okay. This is creative work, stretching beyond your boundaries. Most organizations struggle with this. They will start out this process of talking about what they want to become, but then somebody will raise a hand and say, "Well, we can't really do that because of this." And then somebody else will say, "Well, we can't really do that because this other thing is going to happen." And pretty soon, it becomes a tactical exercise. They miss the point.

For this exercise, table all talk about what the obstacles are going to be. You will plug those back in later, working from your history and your analysis of the current situation.

### Imagine a Future Without Obstacles

I suggest you actually write out a few paragraphs describing this business without obstacles. Touch on all aspects of your business:

- Finances
- Operations
- Leadership
- Staff
- Communications
- Types of customers

Take everything we have considered and apply it to what is in your future. In your wildest dreams, if you could create anything in your business, what would it be?

This exercise gets at why your business is relevant to its target market. That is what ties your history to your future—your relevancy to what your customers need and want. If you do not pay attention to this, you risk becoming irrelevant, either by getting too focused on cost, or letting yourself get into a "me-too" position.

To complete this "no obstacles" exercise, start connecting the dots between that utopian future and where you are today. Where do you see yourself one year, three years, five years, and ten years into the future?

### Can Anyone be Creative?

*The "no obstacles" exercise requires creativity. But can everyone really be creative? Yes. Creativity is an innate behavior—look at any 5-year-old. He can bend the laws of physics (in his mind). Icebreaker games can be used to tap into the inner child; these can be very helpful with a group of leaders working on the "obstacles" exercise.*

**KNOW THIS**

Sony presents a good example of a company that went from the leading edge in relevance to irrelevance. When Sony introduced the Walkman it was a breakthrough product. It was relevant in a whole new way. Sony created a product that filled a need their customers did not know they had—music on the go. Sony ruled the market for several decades. Then along came the MP3 player that could store thousands of songs and sort and shuffle them in myriad ways. Suddenly a portable machine that just played pre-recorded tapes was irrelevant. All your music now fits on something the size of postage stamp. That is a total game changer.

Successful companies are already envisioning two years down the road, imagining what is going to be next. Apple is a company that from a technology standpoint, always seems to be looking not just into tomorrow, but what is next, two or three years from now.

What technology is going to change your world, and what new equipment will it require? If you are not looking at that today, what is going to happen in the future when shifts occur?

If that is a little overwhelming to think about, take a deep breath. Pause and think about the ground we have covered. It all contributes to the Direction of your company. Now might be a good time to look back at your notes on your vision, mission, and values, to see what might have become clearer to you as you considered your company's compelling story, history, industry trends, and where you envision your company going, if all obstacles were removed. As I said earlier, you can't really finalize the Direction without taking all these aspects of your business into account, with deep thought and discussion among the leadership that leads to realization of the unique selling points that comprise your competitive difference.

## Great Leaders Required

The company's leaders are responsible for steering the firm in the direction of its vision. That requires communicating their passion for that vision, and creating an expectation of accountability at all levels.

It is a lot easier to lead a group of people when everyone has a unified sense of where they are going. When Kennedy made his speech in the early 1960s that by the end of the decade the U.S. would have a man on the moon, it was a very clear and concise message. A lot of people bought into that concept and we were able to achieve that goal. Consider how that goal required everything we have been talking about: committed leaders, a clear sense of direction, well-defined values. When you think about what NASA accomplished in the 1960s with the technology of the time, it's pretty amazing.

That direction required the right people in the right places, doing the right things at the right time and for the right purpose. To get to that point, you need great leadership.

It is that mentality of strong leadership that makes a company into a Golden Apple. That culture starts at the top and works its way down from there. If it is not happening at the highest level in the organization, it is very difficult to hold the staff accountable.

I think that each individual in the leadership group working on vision needs to understand their role on the leadership team, and understand their own personal vision— what they personally want to accomplish in life.

We all have a desire to be purposeful in some way, shape or form. The clearer we understand our purpose, our strengths, and how we fit into the organization, the better we perform. That comes down to the senior leadership role. Is that leader aligning his team with the vision? Is he putting the right people in the right positions? Is he communicating, "You are good at this. This is why you are here. This is what I need you to focus on." A good leader presents a model of a culture in which ego and competition have no place.

### Leaders Leave a Legacy

*Powerful leaders create legacy—in other words, they create a culture that will continue beyond their tenure. Secure and confident leaders know the importance of leaving a legacy intact.*

The clearer the individual leaders are on personal vision, the easier it is for the leadership group to create a company vision. If individuals do not understand how they impact the organization, they will fail to understand their purpose. We all strive to have purpose and we are far more productive when working from our strengths. Think of a job you were in where you did not clearly understand your role or how what you did impacted your company. How did that affect you personally? Also consider what happened when you

### Direction Requires the Right People in the Right Roles

*Achieving competitive differentiation through direction demands that you examine the fit of the people you have to the roles you have them in. Leaders must understand not to hire clones. Too often I see the leaders bring in people just like themselves because, from a personality standpoint, it is much easier to get along with them. There is a lot less conflict. But actually you want a degree of conflict within your leadership team. You want people who will push each other to take the company further in the direction of its vision. We will take up this topic in chapter 6 on the third task of a Golden Apple company: People.*

were given duties that did not match your strengths. Did it make your job easier or was it more difficult? Was it your best work when roles and duties were misaligned?

## Customer Impact

What is the impact of your company culture on your customers? Customers want you to talk about your products and services in a meaningful way.

First, let's define "meaningful." What is meaningful is what moves you, makes you feel an emotion, like loyalty or desire. How do emotions help you talk about your products and services in a meaningful way? Here is where social media has helped.

Consumers are interacting with brands more now than ever. They can go online and write reviews. They can give their own input on a particular product or service. Creating a meaningful message is not just something a marketer does anymore—the fact is, your customers are doing it for you as well.

### Interact with Your Customers
First, learn what customers are saying about you. Often this can be discovered online. Social media has opened up ways to learn what others think about your services and clue you in to what might need to change. A simple step is to set up Google Alerts. Setting alerts for your business name can help you uncover what people are searching for. Find ways to connect with individuals so you can get direct feedback. Address any comments or concerns when they are discovered. Thank people for their praises, and follow up with less positive responses.

**KNOW THIS**

Travel sites are a good example. If you go on Travelocity™ or Expedia™ or a similar travel sites and you are looking for a hotel, one of the first things you are going to see is a rating scale. That rating was not assigned by the travel site— it is done by people who have stayed in a particular hotel. They share their own feedback on how well or how poorly the hotel performed.

Feedback has even moved into the product realm. I just bought a new camera from Best Buy™. Afterward they sent me a message inviting me to go online and rate the performance. They were actively asking me to participate in how the product I bought is perceived. We are seeing a lot more of this happening.

There are organizations whose purpose is to rate specific products and services. In the health care field, there are now services that allow you to rate the physician you just saw. Before, the only way you found out if a product was good or bad was if your neighbor bought one and talked about it, or if there was a consumer recall on it that was publicly announced—and many happen with only the people affected getting that information, and the public would never know about it.

*Consumer Reports* came in many years ago to be the unbiased voice, not supported by advertising, to give honest product reviews. The company has prided itself on doing standardized testing and then making a judgment based on the facts. The difference we are now seeing is that consumers are getting involved and taking a subjective approach to product rating. You have people who will speak highly and a number who will bash a product, some because they were truly disappointed by it and others because they are loyal brand fans of some other product.

My point is this: Your marketing department cannot control your customer impact. They can only influence it. Only your company culture can live up to what marketing promises. When everyone in the company is aligned with your vision, mission, and values—when everyone believes in and conveys the same compelling story—the impact on your customers is tremendous. They will experience your competitive difference every time they touch your company.

> ### Use the Internet to Connect with Customers
> *In today's market, people want to "connect" with your company. The Internet gives people ways to interact with you like never before. It is important to understand how to use this tool.*

## *Who is the Right Customer?*

Your ideal customers will be like the customers you serve now—some of them. Base your image of the ideal customer on the ones who:

- You enjoy working with
- Pay their bills
- Reduce your "pain" factor
- Are located where you can serve them efficiently

In other words, who can you turn into "raving fans"—the kind of people who advocate for your products or services because they are just so darned delighted with the solutions you deliver and the way you deliver them?

## Conclusion

Finding a "true north," a Direction by which to navigate, is the first task of a Golden Apple company. Having a firmly-grounded sense of Direction allows the company to align its resources toward specific goals, easily identifying that which helps it move forward and that which merely distracts.

In this chapter we have examined your vision, mission, and values, in order to translate them into a compelling story. We have studied the "history lesson" of your past performance, considered current trends, and what ideal future you could set your sights on. All of these aspects I have asked you to think about come together to comprise your company's culture, from which competitive differentiation arises.

In the previous chapter, I gave you a taste of the success factors that will come your way once you complete all five tasks of a Golden Apple company—among them, increased profits, lower costs, greater stability, and easier recruiting of the best talent. To achieve these gains, all that is required is commitment.

In this chapter I have laid out the important work you must commit to; work that will guide every strategic decision ahead as we make our way through the next task: mapping your Path.

## Chapter

# 5

# The Second Task of the Golden Apple: The Path

In the last chapter, I used the highway analogy to convey how you first choose a destination—your Direction—and then commit to a route to get there—your Path. This is the aspect of your business that works with your mission statement to turn it into a strategic plan that is truly actionable.

Your Path is the highway you use to get from point A to point B. Your Path describes, in detail, the strategies and goals that make up the process of getting to the outcomes you want. Your Path tells you where you need to make the turns. What roads are you going to take? When are you going to know if you are veering off that route? How will you know when it is time to ask yourself, "Is this a change we need to make, or is it a distraction? If so, what do we have to do to get back on course?"

Choosing your Path demands innovation. If you are taking the same route everybody else is taking, you are going to end up in a "me too" position all along the way. It's okay that you share the same direction, but how you get there needs to have something original about it, something unique to your company. That is how innovation becomes part of the Path.

### Innovation and the Path

By now you know I think innovation is a critical aspect of competitive differentiation. Your ability to differentiate depends on your ability to innovate on every one of the five tasks of the Golden Apple.

Companies that develop an innovative culture can differentiate themselves from their competitors, even if they are producing a product or service so widely used that it is becoming commoditized (buyers perceive little or no value difference between competing offerings). One company will always be the perceived leader. The task of finding your Path is about ways you can take action to become that perceived leader. Nine times out of ten that comes from the role of innovation in the corporate culture you have created.

**KNOW THIS**

### On the Road
*Direction is your compass; Path is your highway.*

Many companies talk about how innovative they are, but when you look at the cultural aspects of the company, they are not as innovative as they think. There might be a few innovators within the company, but for the most part, across the company, there are not that many people embracing innovation because the leadership does not embrace it either. As a leader, creating a culture of innovation is ultimately up to you.

### Innovation in My Consulting Practice

If you would asked me two years ago if I would have an office in China, I would have said, "no way." So why am I doing business in China today?

I developed this business strategy as a response to the degree of competition in the coaching and strategy development area I was working in. If I just operated in my city, I would face a lot of competition. I asked myself, "What are the aspects that would separate me, in this market, that could open up some new doors?" I researched the question. What I got out of that was, "If you were to take an international approach, there are not a lot of people competing for that." It allowed me to expand in a way that was cost-effective for me. Considering factors of resource and time available to me, what was it that I could do? China has had an open market to the west for quite a few years; there is a lot of growth there, and a lot of perceived opportunities. How could I take what I do and what I am good at, organizational development, and use it to leverage the opportunities in China? I discovered I could help companies here develop strategic plans for exporting. I just needed to surround myself with the right people.

Opportunities exist, if you understand the business culture in China. I sought out Chinese people who speak English fluently to help me learn how to go about doing business in China. My business, like many, involves trading dollars for hours. At some point I max out the hours I can make available. So part of my process was figuring out how I could expand my business by leveraging the expertise of other people. I have people on both the U.S. and the Chinese sides, the right resources to provide strategic planning and organizational development to people doing business with China.

My strategic goal was to specialize, not generalize. I wanted managed, controlled, focused growth. I am growing my business organically, nurturing it, as opposed to just running out and tackling opportunities full-on, because of the impact that would have on my financial resources.

## My Mastermind Group: Another Example of Innovation Strategy

Someone in my Mastermind group emailed me recently saying he finds my thinking far ahead of most people. My use of my Mastermind group is a strategy for personal and professional growth; it's part of my strategy for innovation. I use the group to gather and understand new data, new information. There is value for you to connect with like-minded people, inside or outside, of your industry. Trade associations are good. Even though you might be among competitors, you can learn from each other and help each other's business grow.

If sharing information with competitors sounds like a bad approach to you, check your world view. Do you view the world with abundance or scarcity? Those who take the abundant approach are

### *Join a Mastermind Group*

**KNOW THIS**

*A Mastermind groups offer a combination of peer brainstorming, education, accountability and support in a group setting to sharpen your business and personal skills. A mastermind group helps its members achieve success. To find a group or create your own, visit apples2applesbook.com.*

open to learning from other people, even if there is a certain degree of competition. On the other hand, to those with a scarcity perspective, everything's a trade secret. "We do not help anybody else out; we do not talk to competitors." This is where the Mastermind group comes in. When you have professionals, like-minded in wanting to learn from each other and develop others, you are creating the climate for innovation in your own business.

## Your Business: Obstacles and All

In the last chapter I asked you to envision your business without obstacles. Now, reality sets in. You face certain obstacles and challenges on your path; you bring with you certain strengths and advantages, as well as weaknesses, on the trip. You either work through these or work around them to get as close to that ultimate outcome that you want.

Your path is a work in progress. There are times you are going to have to take a detour, or face a stretch of bumpy road. If you acquire the necessary resources, you can work your way through the obstacles to overcome your challenges. But we first have to identify all the factors that are going to get in the way, internal and external.

In the highway metaphor, the idea is to keep the vehicle in motion, headed in the right direction, on the right route. If you do that you are going to get a lot closer to the end result you want to achieve versus just sitting in the car in idle, or worse yet, taking any path hoping that random choices will get you to where you want to go.

This brings us to analysis of the internal and external factors affecting your business. Internal factors are what is within your four walls in the context of your business—what is under your control. External factors are everything in the environment beyond your walls, everything over which you have no control, but that directly impacts on your success. To complete the second task of the Golden Apple, you need an in-depth understanding of these influencing factors.

It's time for another exercise. This time, instead of imagining your business without obstacles, I will ask you to look at obstacles up close. You may choose to use the SWOT analysis or any other technique. The problem with SWOT—and I have been just as guilty of this as most other facilitators—is that it does not guide you to a clear breakdown of what exactly you should be looking at. The question is thrown out—what are your strengths? What are your weaknesses, opportunities and threats? But with no more guidance than that, the result is just a brainstorming session to create a list of everything that comes to mind. Typically something gets missed. You do not necessarily have all the right people in the room at the time. It's easy to overlook something just because it lies outside the expertise of the people in the planning session.

If you do not look at your situation by category, you are very likely to miss something. For that reason, I like to use the planning tool shown in Figure 5.1. Let's zoom in a little closer on what I mean by each of these terms; then you can try the exercise of working through this self-analysis on your own or with your leadership team.

## Figure 5-1 Influencing Factors and Your Path

| | Internal Factors (Under your control) | | External Factors (Influences beyond your control) | |
|---|---|---|---|---|
| | Strengths | Challenges | Strengths | Challenges |
| Direction | | | | |
| Leadership | | | | |
| Culture | | | | |
| Talent | | | | |
| Operations | | | | |
| Money | | | | |
| Time | | | | |
| Logistics | | | | |
| Technology | | | | |
| Innovation | | | | |
| Marketing | | | | |
| Other | | | | |
| Beyond your control | | | | |

## Influencing Factors

Internal or external, each of the factors listed in Figure 5.1 is exerting an influence on your business right now, and will continue to do so in the future. This is your moment to create awareness of just how each influencing factor is affecting you.

### Direction

As I have said elsewhere, Direction is your vision of what your company can become; it is what aligns your resources to achieve that desired condition. If you are fuzzy on what external and internal Direction factors might be, read Chapter 4.

*Leadership*

What are your strengths related to leadership? What are some of the challenges that you have related to that? How does the leadership of your competitors impact you?

*Culture*

What about your culture works really, really well? Those are influences you want to keep. What about your culture does not work at all or does not align with where you want to take you organization? Those are influencing factors you need to change.

Let me bring in an example from my work with a four-year school that is part of the state university system. I worked with this school on strategic planning. The institution needed to make a major shift from the typical state college model, where tuition and state funds drive the income for the university, because the state funds are going down and that trend is going to continue downward for the foreseeable future. With less funding coming in from the state, and you cannot automatically increase tuition to make up the gap, you have to find other ways to take what has essentially been a public sector model (funding through taxes) and make it more of a private sector model. In my work with the leadership we realized we had to take a more entrepreneurial direction. They have to find other ways to acquire revenue besides the two sources they had relied on, which is through the student body and through the state government. My work is getting them to think dynamically. I have a senior leader who understands the need to do this, but many of the professors and other adjuncts underneath him are still stuck in a hundred-year-old way of doing business. In terms of their culture, they should be working on a paradigm shift to move them forward, because the environment around them has changed.

*Talent*

What are your strengths or challenges regarding the people in your company? This is about making sure that you have a good fit for the positions and that you know how to best lead and develop those individuals. Ideally, you have your talent doing the right things at the right time for the right reasons.

How are you communicating so everyone stays aligned on Direction and Path? How are you empowering the individuals to then take that information and innovate?

Returning to the example of the college, their analysis of the need for a shift in culture brought up a need for change in their talent pool as well. Their talent is essentially the faculty who teach in the university. They are in an academic model that has existed for a century. It is never been a research school; they have not had a grant-writing department to specifically focus on gaining additional funding. This means a shift in talent is called for because now they have got to get people who are grant-writers and they have to get projects going that are grantable.

Another initiative involves collaborating with alumni who have gone on to open their own businesses or work with other businesses. Here is a chance to use the talent pool of the university to go out and do projects with the private sector. There is potential to do business in a way that increases revenue and allows them to continue growing the university. And that is a completely different shift than just developing expertise in grant-writing. It is finding other resources outside of that.

One issue I go through when I do this exercise with clients, talking about talent, is to assess how the client group is functioning with regards to training and development. This is where leaders start creating more of an emotional connection, to get people to start wanting to make the changes that leaders see as necessary.

If change is something that is dictated by the leadership, it can easily be lost because there might be a buy-in from individuals on a rational level, but is there buy-in on an emotional level? People need both rational and emotional buy-in to be motivated to actually make the change happen. Fail to get that buy-in, that emotional connection, and you will either lose your talent or watch them become ineffective.

As you consider your talent, think about both internal and external groups, because each group influences the company in some way. Vendors are critical because they are an extension of your company. By providing you products and services they are supporting the direction you are going. If you have misalignment there, it is just as bad as if you have misalignment with your staff. If you have a vendor that is not producing quality and you are differentiating on quality, you have got a problem. Again, we are talking about right fit. How does that vendor fit into your organization? And sometimes, the independent contractors are the most difficult ones to deal with.

Talent is a topic we will cover in more detail in Chapter 6 coming up.

### Operations

How do your processes take place? Where can you streamline or innovate? Consider not just your operational processes, but even the management processes by which you go about creating and improving processes. At this level you are looking at how you go about redefining or making processes more efficient. Operations ties into the process issues I will talk about in Chapter 7.

### Money

How is your business set for internal capital? Can you fund your own growth? Do you need to borrow for growth? In many cases, borrowing can be very challenging if the ratios on the balance sheet do not fit what traditional banks are looking for. There are other resources, such as venture capital, but the right fit can also be difficult to find there. If you do not have internal capital or the kind of past performance banks are looking for, you really have to get creative to figure out how you are going to fund growth. It might take you longer to get to where you are going, but it does not necessarily mean you have to stop what you are doing.

If you have access to capital, you can have an accelerated time-line and ambitious plans. Less access to capital? Okay, now you are going to have to deal with a longer time frame.

### Time

Where is the window of opportunity for the next steps in your business? It is the nature of business today that things move at an extremely fast pace. For example, if you have come up with an innovative new product, and you cannot bring that product or service to sell soon enough, you might miss your window of opportunity. Is there a way you can leapfrog over a competitor instead of asking how are you catching up with your competition?

Desktop publishing presents a good example of how quickly processes can change, creating opportunity for some while taking it away from others. Look at what small businesses today are able to do in-house to make professional-quality documents. In years past they would have farmed out graphics work to somebody else and would have paid a good price for it. Now the laser printers you have in your office can do a reasonably good job. Most people do not notice the difference. This is where the quality issue could become a non-differentiator because the end-user does not know and does not care about the difference. In-house graphics work is saving money for a lot of small businesses, but the transition forced a lot of independent graphics businesses to change their model.

I am seeing the same with video production now. Not only are the video cameras available at consumer prices really good, the editing software is now available that anyone can use. With the right software you just plug in the camera, download the video you took, and in a couple of steps you can make it look pretty darn good. Now video producers are changing their business model like the graphic people did when desktop publishing came along. The window of opportunity for business innovation, especially in technology, can be really tight. Your business strategy might be able to leverage that to your advantage, or it might be a significant challenge your Path must respond to.

*Technology*

How is technology going to affect your business in the future? Is technology an advantage for you or is it going to pass you by? Plenty of businesses have seen the technology they were most known for yesterday have to shift so they can be around tomorrow.

You can buy technology or you can "rent"–that is, rely on outside suppliers who take on the risks and rewards so you don't have to. Apple innovates some core product developments, but they seek outside vendors to innovate the chips for their products, and to innovate the glass for their screens. You could follow that model for your technology, or you could see an opportunity to differentiate from competitors by keeping the technology internal to your company, and make it a core value of your culture.

*Logistics*

How do you deliver your product or service? Taking a look at my own business, back when the Internet was in a fledgling stage, the speed of data transfer made doing business online difficult. So for me, coaching or offering any sort of planning services remotely to another part of the country or the world would have been extremely difficult. Business would have to be handled by a conference call with no interaction between the client and me other than by voice. Today, I have clients I can work with anywhere in the world, and I can transfer documents instantly. I can pull up video, they can see me and I can see them. That is a game changer for many service-related businesses. We can cut out the airline fees and a number of travel expenses if the client is willing to work with us using the technology.

Logistics have shifted from physically moving people around and at the same time, logistics have shifted from physically moving documents around. You can upload and download files or share documents using online tools.

Logistics could be about growing from a local business to an international business. Are you interested in doing business overseas? If you have to move your product from one town to the next, that is easy enough. But when you have to move your product out of the country, onto a boat, across the ocean, onto a loading platform, and then onto a truck and then distribute it on the other side of the world, how does that change things?

Your challenges and opportunities with logistics depend on the specific industry you are in, but it definitely needs to be looked at, in terms of how what you use or sell gets from point A to point B.

Globalization is great in that now we can all do business everywhere. But, now everybody else can compete with us wherever we are. The logistic piece of it ties very tightly to the technology piece.

### Innovation

How is innovation built into your culture? As I said at the opening of this chapter, you must have innovation built in, or you are going to have no solution when the technology changes, or the logistics, or the procedures that you use to go through the next evolution.

### Marketing

What is your internal understanding of marketing in terms of the company you are trying to create? Marketing has been going through a tremendous shift. It needs examination in terms of strengths, and challenges.

Often, it is handed off to an outside expert to create the marketing platform for you. It is fine to rely on outside experts to do that because most companies do not have the resources they need in an internal marketing department to manage all that. Even those with internal marketing departments still outsource specific tasks.

At the leadership level there needs to be an internal understanding of how the nature of marketing has changed, especially with the movement away from print and traditional media, into the sphere of social media.

It has become even more critical today to build relationships with your customers and connect with your customers in a different way than you have in the past. That requires a certain degree of expertise in-house. As a result, your company may need some education and understanding about that.

This exercise of self-analysis on the many factors influencing your business, internal and external, should heighten your awareness of where your business faces challenges and where you have opportunities for meaningful competitive differentiation.

> ### *Keep Creating the Compelling Story In-House*
> *Creating your compelling story—that unique message that conveys your vision—is not something you can outsource to a marketing firm. If you allow somebody else to create that for you, what do they have to draw on? They do not work for you. They have not spent any significant amount of time with you, digging into what your company is all about. You are leaving it to somebody else to decide what you are. To me, that is scary, because they are likely to come up with whatever they think will be the best choice for them, on your behalf.*

**DO THIS**

From the internal standpoint, it is really about understanding in very real terms what your organization is today. Good or bad, internal factors are those over which you have full control.

Because you cannot change anything until you are realistic about what you have now, you need to understand these influencing factors to the nth degree. If you lie to yourselves to make it sound better than it actually is, you are going to fail. You need to be totally honest about what needs to change.

### External Analysis: Factors Beyond Your Control

External analysis requires understanding the environment around you and seeing how that is going to influence your Path. You may not be able to change some factors in the external environment, but you can choose a path to steer around them, or use them as inspirations for innovations that leap past competitors.

In terms of your competition, you will likely need to drill into what is going on with each major competitor, one by one. Who is giving you serious competition, and which aspect of what they are doing is making the competition so intense? Are they bombarding your customers with advertising? Did they just bring out a game-changing product? Have they developed a delivery channel solution that leap frogs over your current methods?

What if you come to understand that your market is contracting, perhaps to the point of disappearing entirely? Products have their life cycles. We have seen enough shifts in technology to know that can spell the end to a whole line of business. That does not necessarily mean the end of your opportunities. It might just mean that you need to make a shift in your business.

The biggest example of that in recent years is probably IBM. IBM started out in the early 20th century making business equipment, and as computers came along, they became part of IBM's business. Up until the 1990s and early 2000s, the company still focused on producing computer equipment, such as servers. They have since moved into more of a consulting role. They have gone from a product-based business to a service-based business. Their marketing has changed to reflect that. They build customized business solutions for companies in the Fortune 1000, for the most part. They knew that they were no longer competitive in the marketplace that they had owned for so many years. They scrapped that and picked consulting for their future. New direction, new path—that is how they coped with the reality that their old line of business was not going to sustain them into the future.

## Determining the Best Path

Once you have analyzed all the factors influencing your path, internally and externally, you have got the information you need to choose the strategic path for your business. In terms of competitive differentiation, this all comes together around your pricing strategy.

### Pricing Strategy

In earlier chapters I have said that when price is the only differentiator, the company with the lowest price gets the sale. If you cannot differentiate yourself on features more compelling than price, your product or service has become commoditized. Your only option seems to be "their price minus 10 percent."

To step away from that pitfall, where you are letting competitors set your price, start with internal considerations.

A lot of pricing is actually driven by your company culture. There are instances where two companies make an almost identical product, yet one product is twice as expensive as another, and that company seems to be selling plenty at that price. You have got to look at your price in terms of what you believe is the value you bring to the buyer. I think most companies want to be considered a fair price, but an even greater value.

When you consider your price take into account: What is your ideal profit margin? What is your baseline margin; what you have to make just to break even? The metric we need to look at about pricing is, are you commoditized or are you not? It's not a matter of where you set your price point because in any company, there is going to be argument, should it be higher, should it be lower. No company can grow without some sort of profit, and the more profit you have, the more resources you have for growth, innovation, whatever it is the company needs to move towards your vision.

If you consider your offering to be commoditized, with little or no meaningful differences between your product or service and competitors', that is a warning sign. Something else is not working—something in your messaging, in your product, in your service, in your care for your customer, or the type of customer you are going after. Whatever it is, you have to look at all those factors to discover where commoditization comes in.

The offering that stands out in a commoditized field is the one that is the best fit for the buyer's needs. Which is another way of saying, what problem are you solving? What pain are you getting rid off? As I said in earlier chapters, people seek products or services that remove pain, deliver pleasure, or better yet, both. We always move away from pain and we are trying to move towards pleasure. If you are a better fit than any competing or substitute products, moving customers away from pain and toward pleasure in ways a buyer can clearly articulate, you have achieved true differentiation.

### The Path: A Working Document

The Path your leadership team develops out of this strategic planning process needs to be documented. But that does not mean putting it into a hundred pages or more in a binder somewhere. How do we make this plan into something useful? How do we make it a resource rather than a document that just sits on the shelf?

The answer lies in breaking down the ownership. In many cases, when a strategic plan is created, the executive team pulls in key people from different departments to get a more rounded view of what they plan to do. But it's really about them taking whatever is created and breaking it down into smaller chunks and assigning accountability in the right places to the right people.

**DO THIS**

### Strategic Planning is a Fluid Process

*Too often, planning is a static process. A strategic plan document is created, bound, put on a shelf, and forgotten about because of all the day-to-day stuff going on in the business. The planners have not followed through to make a behavioral change in the organization. You want to get to a different level then you are at now. You cannot achieve that by continuing to do what you have been doing all along. Implement your plan, and treat it as fluid. It should change in response to what you encounter as you put it to work.*

What I have seen is that a plan is typically created; copies are put in binders, and distributed to the CEO, senior officers, and occasionally middle management.

The plan is built into their performance reviews. Everyone is given objectives for the year and that is what they are carrying forward. This is not a bad thing; it is just that those plans are only reviewed once or twice a year, when a performance review comes around. There is nothing that lays out the timeline of certain milestones to be met.

## Drive Strategies Down to Action Steps

When I look at a strategic plan, I focus on how we can take this plan and break it down into bite-size chunks that work towards the change processes called for in the plan. Without breaking it down, it is just overwhelming.

It is like losing weight. If you are looking to lose 50 or 100 pounds, and you just focus on that as your goal, it is going to be de-motivating. But if you focus on losing two pounds in the next seven days, most people can do that. If you focus on that each week, eventually you get to your target. It is the same process with strategic planning. You take your big goals and chunk them down into actions that people can undertake, step by step. Then you make sure that what you are doing, week by week, is working towards those goals.

Strategies break down into goals, which break down into action steps, each with tasks for which a single person is responsible. You are basically trying to drive every goal in that strategic plan down to steps that individuals are responsible for and can take care of in a planning timeframe of a week or two. "What do I need to do in this week ahead of me to make sure we are on the right overall path and on schedule to reach our destination?"

Breaking the plan down into action steps allows you to make sure accountability is in the right places, and making sure people understand what accountability is. Accountability does not mean you are necessarily doing the work. It means you are accountable to make sure that the work gets done. Too many leaders take it upon themselves to say, "Well, I am accountable for it. Therefore, I must do it to make sure it's done right." That is not what this is about. It is about making sure leaders have a point of contact, a manager who is going to be tracking this action, measuring it and making sure that action is staying on target. It is through that individual's team that the work gets done. This is not about just pushing off work to the next layer below you. It is about pushing the right work to the right people.

**KNOW THIS**

## *Leaders Must Engage and Share*

*Leaders may find it difficult to relinquish control. This creates a challenge in the organization. Failing to engage others and share the work results in a lack of training, keeping others from achieving their potential, and leaders overloaded with responsibilities.*

It is also about making sure timeframes are realistic. You need incremental change. This planning process prevents trying to accomplish two years' work in two weeks. Each goal needs to be broken down to action steps that you can follow through on.

### Innovation and the Path

You build in checkpoints to verify that what you are doing is actually progressing toward the goals you have defined. It may be that a new direction has emerged—there can be innovation as we are on this path. This is where you create links between the Path and the Direction—between the strategic plan, driven down to action steps, and your vision. Is this direction you are going in aligned with your vision? If not, what do you need to adjust? Are you on track toward the shorter-term direct measurable goals you are trying to accomplish? Are those short-term goals tied into your values? In other words, are you going to break your values if you continue down the path you are on? Is it going against what you truly believe in? And then from there, what are your critical measures? So if you are doing this, is it relating to those measures you determined were most important to track your success?

### Example: Executive Summit in China

Let me draw an example from my business. Part of my overall strategy is to focus on international growth. Toward that goal I have developed partnerships both here and in China.

Our vision is to help companies have success doing business in China. The pain that we have uncovered is that many companies, while they see the opportunity in China, are fearful because of the different business culture. They are not sure how to work with it.

Others are not afraid but try to work with it in the U.S. style of doing business. Our American way does not necessarily work over there.

The value I am promoting here is our stewardship to our clients—that we are going to take them through this process and protect them and help them along the way to make the process smooth or better and faster than if they did it on their own. We will make it a lot simpler and a lot more profitable.

We are promoting the values of honesty and trust. Its key for me that I make sure that the people I am working with live up to those expectations for our clients. My challenge is to align myself with the right people to know that the work is going to get done, and it is going to get done on time. It is going to get done well. I need to be able to trust that the quality of the output from my international team is going to match or exceed the expectations of the client.

### Assess Before Adapting the Path

*To determine if the direction you are moving is a good one to continue, use the Influencing Factors exercise. If your progress is playing to your strengths, you are going in a good direction—adapt the Path to fit. If your progress is moving you toward increasing challenges, change course and get back to the Path.*

DO THIS

That is the vision. As a goal, I have partnered with a business magazine to host an executive summit in China. Our goal is to take a group of business people to China in the spring of 2011.

We have a solid vision for the trip itself. The whole point of doing this trip—my partners with the magazine and I agree—is to offer meaningful value to the executives who attend the executive summit. That means we have to make prime connections with the right people. We have to bring multiple people from multiple industries together. We have to get them in a forum where they can talk. It is not just a lecture circuit. Our hope is they are going to talk for a short period of time and there is going to be more Q&A. After the Q&A, there will be networking meetings. After the networking meetings, if it makes sense, there will be one-on-one meetings and we will help our business people gain value from those meetings.

These are specific goals that deliver on the vision of the executive summit.

These goals break down into action steps, starting with convincing executives to travel with us. We are advertising the trip through emails to the magazine's subscriber list, linking to it on our websites, writing about it on our blogs. It drives down to specifics—who are we emailing? Who are we writing? Who are we making phone calls to? My actions are tied to selling the seats on the trip because we have to make that reservation by a certain time. And I am also making the phone calls to put together the logistical arrangements.

We are breaking it down to a detailed level, holding the partners in the venture accountable for everyone reaching out to their audience, to let them know the value of the trip. One thing we have discovered is that we need to really get people to understand why it is important for them to go—create the picture of what could happen in their business. This goes back to the pain or pleasure principle—we have to communicate what the pleasure will be. They will gain access to new markets, have new points of differentiation, and other assets like that.

## Investment

By the time you have completed your analysis of influencing factors, and determined the best path based on those factors, you should have a very detailed idea of what your whole plan entails. Now you have to tie that to what it takes to accomplish it, which is to say, money and time. Whether you have access to money or not influences how quickly you can implement the plan. Now is the time to think realistically about whether the timeline you have created is realistic for what you are trying to achieve. Is there enough ROI available on that timeline to make the effort worth the cost?

If you are trying to make a million dollars in the next 12 months, do you have the resources to make it happen in that short timeframe? Are you setting yourselves up for failure? If you are looking to make a million dollars in 12 months, you had better have the right service or product coming in to the market, at the right time. You had better have the right message, know who your audience is, and then have the resources to reach that audience so you can achieve your goal. You have to gauge based on the investment—is it going to achieve the goal you want, on the timeline you want? If not, you might have to recalibrate your investment. At this point there is interplay between the goals, the timeline and the resources available. This is an iterative process requiring you to develop the plan up to a point, and then touch on the investment question. You take a reality check and maybe scale back your plans.

I think it's always important to have a stretch goal, something that encourages you to be visionary, to reach for something emotionally compelling.

If you are going to reach that big goal—what do you need to do to make sure it happens? Focus on resources. The three biggest ones are going to be time, money, and talent. To get other resources usually involves one of these three. If you are lacking one or more of these resources, I would not necessarily say you need to scale back. I would still be asking the question, "What do you need to do to make that happen?" Once you figure that out ask, "Is this realistic, given where you are today?" Then ask what you can do to make the stretch goal realistic. What would you have to do or do differently?

---

### What, Me Worry?

*In order to achieve your goals, you need to be concerned with the three critical investments of Time, Money and Talent. While other details are important, you cannot accomplish your goals without first addressing your skills, the spend, and the time it takes to get the job done.*

---

In most cases, it comes down to the question of what you are willing to give up now to gain that success later on. That is a difficult question for many people to answer because they do not want to give up anything. Going back to the weight loss example, why don't more people lose weight on diets? What does a diet do? It usually takes away the things that you enjoy most and gives you the things that you usually like the least. Any time you take something away from people mentally, it triggers wanting it all that much more.

This question of investment is really about understanding where you want go, how you want to get there, and how to reach your targets, without being unrealistic about what you are able to give up in the short-term.

## Target Market

Now that you have examined all the influencing factors affecting your choice of a Path for your business, considered the strategic action steps driven by that plan, and evaluated the investment required to adopt that plan, are you ready to implement it? Not yet. Now that you know the Path you want to take, it is time to focus on the customers who will be your target market. Does this Path lead you toward a customer base sufficient to make the sales you need?

When it comes to defining your target market, you have to drill down a mile deep and only go an inch wide. It is more efficient and effective than trying to be all things to all people, which usually means you are nothing to nobody. No one understands what you really do that separates you from your competition and then you are competing on price. Back to square one.

You have to be laser-sharp and focused on the market you can serve better than anyone else. If you are not perceived as the best you are diluted amongst your competition, stuck in the middle of the bell curve. When you are the best in your industry, you can choose to focus on a particular niche or a group of industries.

You can consciously choose your target market or let luck and timing play a role. Going into the dental industry was not my choice originally; it was completely a fluke. I got referred into one firm where there was a need. That client then referred me to another person who had a similar need, and pretty soon I am working with a group of people in that industry and find out there is a huge need there. I found a huge opportunity. Many companies that have been successful tripped into their market one way or another. They found something that worked and then were able to capitalize on it.

This is one of the areas where there is real serendipity in business. But remember the saying, "Luck favors the prepared mind." You have to know your Direction, be clear about your vision and values, before you can tell a good target market from a distraction.

You need to focus on specific markets, but you also need to be nimble enough to know when those markets are rising or falling. You need to be diversified enough that you will not be hurt by challenges within a specific market niche, but you are specialized enough that you are not diluted. To find that sweet spot go back to the problem you solved for your buyers. How did you move your customers from pain toward pleasure?

If you are doing this "Path" work right, you will find a target market that is tightly defined. People have trouble believing they are not letting opportunities slip through their fingers when they do this. Believe me—you are not leaving money on the table when you choose to focus on a tightly defined target market.

The more you are tightly focused on a target market, the more the referrals that come will be a good fit for you as well. In Chapter 3, I said, "If you want to stop letting others drive your price, you will have to stop thinking about price and start thinking about fit."

## Cultural Impact

Once you have completed your analysis of internal and external factors affecting your business, and determined the best path given factors of investment and fit to target markets, I have got one more exercise for you. Consider the impact on your company's culture of following the Path you have chosen.

During business downturns, like the one we went through in 2008-2010, we heard a lot of businesses talk about how they made their operations more efficient. But then you hear people talking and you realize it was not really that they made operations more efficient; they just let people go because they could not afford to keep them on. That meant they loaded the work that those people had been doing onto the people who remained. That did not necessarily mean they were more efficient—it only meant they had reduced their staff.

**DO THIS**

### *Reducing Staff Does Not Increase Productivity*
*Reducing workforce does not automatically equate to increased productivity. Review your processes regularly; the systems by which you operate will need to be optimized each time there is a change in staffing. Read more about process optimization in Chapter 7.*

The difference is whether what you have done is sustainable and energizes your business, or just a short-term gain that is not sustainable in the long term. The impact on company culture of shifting more work onto fewer people is terrible. It is very demoralizing. It is not a sustainable approach. It may work as a response in a crisis but you cannot continue to drive down that path.

Operational efficiency goes back to the question of capacity. If you are at 90 percent or more capacity you do not have capacity to grow. You are going to plateau and eventually you are going to lose business because you can no longer support growth. When you reduce your work force without changing any other factors, you have decreased your capacity. You have no margin on which to grow. That is going to have an impact on your company's culture.

Take, for example, the companies that have designed themselves around an exit strategy. Their goal with bringing in funding is to create an environment for growth in a five- to seven-year business model with the intention that they either have a public stock offering at the end of that time period or a bigger company will buy them out. The leaders plan on cashing in their chips and either starting another business or sitting on a beach for the rest of their lives. If that is your business model it is a short-term plan because there is not anything about sustainability beyond that end-game.

> ### *Hire Carefully to Maintain Alignment*
> *Changing direction constantly will waste time and cause staff to lose focus. Any change should align with vision, mission, and values. Hire executives who will carefully analyze any major shift rather than change for ego's sake.*

Usually the leaders are kept on for a certain period of time to help with any transition measures that need to take place, but in that model typically the old regime moves on. It is rare if they ever stick around with that company for more than a couple of years.

The new owners of the business are left to implement a new culture over the old one. Very few companies have figured out how to do that.

The Path you choose for your business, as far as the strategies and goals that carry you toward your final destination, should be sustainable in its impact on your company's culture. When you are looking at decisions such as how to maintain your growth capacity, or deal with a recessionary business cycle, or how the owners are going to make their exit from the company, keep the cultural impact in mind.

### Seek Feedback

The businesses that innovate are those with a culture of abundance. The businesses that are constantly out there asking the questions, getting the feedback, talking to people, collaborating—they are the ones that grow. More can be accomplished by getting a group of people together and working the problem than can be accomplished by one person working alone. The different inputs, experiences, thought processes equal a sum that is greater than its parts.

The other place you look is to your customers. I am not a huge fan of customer surveys or service satisfaction forms because the information you get is usually influenced by how you ask the questions. You can ask questions that are directive, and get the answer you want to get. Or you can ask a question that gets no answer, and let that say that nothing is wrong. Just because people are not complaining does not mean they are going to come back and do business with you again.

How can you get customer loyalty? Satisfaction is one thing. Am I satisfied? Maybe yes, maybe no. There is a huge difference between satisfactory and great. Satisfactory might just mean "least bad."

What people do differs from what they say or even how they think they behave. People will tell you anything based on the incentive they are getting. A lot of surveys involve some kind of incentive to get the response rate up. Will the respondent bite the hand that feeds him? Probably not. When it comes to product reviews, consider the source. *Consumer Reports* is cleaner than *Motor Trends*. *Consumer Reports* is a nonprofit that does not take advertising. *Motor Trends* will tend to endorse products from major advertisers.

Your group of peers will give you answers that are less biased than a customer survey. For me, it really comes back to what information can you collect internally? You need to look at the data you already have. What do you look at internally? Now maybe you will need to hire outside help to interpret the data. But most of the data you need already exists within your sales data. What do you have and how do you collect it?

You can ask a customer if he will come back and buy again, and you might get the answer you want to hear, but what data backs that up? Surveys are more helpful if there is a high degree of trust between the business and the customer.

More importantly, focus on the key indicators to measure if you are successfully accomplishing your goals. If, for example, you see increased customer referrals, your measure for "client delight" is reporting a healthy trend. That is solid feedback you can steer by.

## The Path: Conclusion

You need to articulate your path in terms of direction, and the end goal because you want to take the easiest route from here to there. That easiest route is going to depend on finding what boosts your business and what in the environment puts the wind at your back, so to speak, because these aspects give you forward momentum. They leverage what is already working well in your company. The easiest way to get from here to there is to choose a path that plays to your strengths.

# Chapter

# 6

# The Third Task of the Golden Apple: People

Your people create your brand. They are the ones who give your customers an experience to remember—or to forget. They are the ones who do what needs to be done to make you succeed, or on the flip side of the coin, fail to do the right things at the right times for the right reasons, and cause your business to fall short.

To run your business effectively and efficiently, you need people who share your vision, mission, and values. You need people who believe in the compelling story and are always ready to talk about it.

In a sense, the "People" task is the most important of the five tasks of the Golden Apple Company. It is people who buy into the Direction. It is people who accept responsibility for the many tasks that make up the Path. It is people who develop and execute the Processes. It is people who create the results for which you develop Measures.

> **KNOW THIS**
>
> **People Power**
> Though the third task in sequence, "People" are the most important and have the most impact on the other tasks.

The job of a company's leader is to put the right people in the right seats on the bus, doing the right things, to cite the metaphor Jim Collins used throughout his book, *Good to Great*. Getting people doing the right thing comes down to communication. How are you communicating your company's vision, mission, and strategic goals? Are you providing that direction and that path with such clarity that individuals can be innovative, as they carry the company forward? Do they know the values of the company well enough to keep the business profitable, efficient, and focused on what it needs to do to grow, no matter which of the seats they happen to fill?

**DO THIS**

### Convey How Roles Impact the Company
*Most people do not understand how their role directly impacts the company. Make sure everyone from the Executive Vice President to the custodian understands the value and purpose of their role.*

To answer these questions, I take my clients through an assessment of their talent, from the leadership team through the many staff roles that must be filled.

## Talent Assessment

In this chapter we will look at how you understand and manage the talent you have at the leadership level, followed by consideration of your staff team. We will consider how you attract and retain top talent, and how you use training to keep everyone in the organization aligned with your overall direction. Finally, we will look at the impacts of making change a consistent part of your company culture—because in today's business world, change is a constant. It may be uncomfortable at times, but if you cannot get your talent prepared to take change in stride, you do not have the right talent on your team.

### Behavioral Profiling: Management Tool or Mistake?

Everybody on your team, from the top leaders' circle to the newest intern, comes to you with a particular personality and set of behaviors. To get the right people on board, and put them in positions that suit their talents and personalities, you need some insight into their psychology. Behavioral profiling has become a standard business tool for gathering information about a person based on

> ### Create an Environment for Talent to Thrive
> *Creating an environment that attracts talent is key. Marine biologists sink ships off the Florida coast to create artificial reefs to provide a healthy environment where fish can thrive. What are you doing to create an environment for talent to thrive?*

DO THIS

observed or self-reported characteristics. You have probably heard of Myers-Briggs Type Indicator (MBTI) profiling, or DISC, which stands for Dominance, Influence, Steadiness, and Conscientiousness. There are several of these kinds of profiling tools available; maybe you have used them in the past. All these systems work on research findings from psychology that group personalities into personality styles (usually four), then match individuals to the styles to assess the extent to which they possess characteristics of each.

We each possess all four traits; we just possess them at different levels. We are stronger in some areas, weaker in others. Armed with this knowledge, managers can better predict behavior individually and within teams.

> ### Learn About to Behavioral Profiling
> *Are behavioral assessment tools a new concept to you? Learn more online. Use the search phrase "behavioral assessment tools for business" and you will find current tools to read about and evaluate.*

DO THIS

Leaders who understand how their employees see the world are better able to match them to the right roles, responsibilities, and assignments, and to engage them at the highest level, for the good of the individual and of the organization. That is a big gain and a good reason to incorporate some kind of behavioral assessments into your company's strategy for managing people.

The important thing I stress with assessment tools is that these are just tools to help you determine what tasks or roles are going to be the best fit for a particular individual. Some people use behavioral profiling tools in the hiring process. I am not a fan of using these tools in hiring decisions. Too often the test is used to put individuals in a box. They are typed as if they are going to behave one way and only this one way all the time. The reality is there are variables and factors that also come into play that no test can account for.

To build a culture of innovation, consider each individual's personal experience, work history, and abilities and strengths. When a combination of individuals with a combination of personalities are allowed to push and pull on each other and engage in discussion and dialogue and conflict—that is how you get true innovation. Use a behavioral profiling as a tool only if it helps you get there.

## Leadership

Let's start our talent assessment at the top: your leadership. A leader has to be someone who takes the wheel and keeps that car between the lines and out of the ditch.

When I am working with an organization, before we even start developing a business plan, the first thing I ask is, "What is your commitment to really doing this?" That is because anytime you are implementing a new plan, you are implementing a change process.

Change can be difficult. I have worked with a number of companies where individuals gave me their commitment upfront, but when the hard work started, all of a sudden, what sounded easy was not anymore. That is why it is important for the executive team to reflect on commitment at the start. "Are we really committed to doing this? When the going gets tough and people push back, how are we going to respond?" Because the push-back will happen.

In any change process there comes a point where people push back. How are you going to deal with that? And are you going to point the finger to blame it on something else or are you going to point the finger right back at the individual who failed to follow through on commitments?

### Commitment and Accountability

Absolutely essential is a leader who exhibits commitment and accountability. You cannot expect to see these values in the staff unless they see it modeled from the leadership level. It is hard to build a company from the bottom up without the support of the top.

Let me give you an example. At one point a company had brought me in to do some training and coaching with their people. They were looking for a positive change in performance, and brought me in to help them achieve that.

I had no trouble convincing them to hire me because top leadership seemed to support the performance coaching initiative. As we were finishing up the contracting conversation, discussing whom I was going to be working with and what I was going to do, I said, "I really want to include the leadership in this process because that is a very important component in making sure the employees understand what the expectations are." If the boss is going through the change process at the same time as the staff, they see that there is commitment from the leaders. In that meeting the feedback I got was, "No, we don't have the time. We just want you to work with our staff and help them become better at what they are doing."

I responded that I would be doing a bit more follow-up to make sure that I communicated to the leaders about what I am working with the staff on and what progress they are making. I said, "What I need from you is to follow up with your staff on accountability. You need to make sure that this stuff is happening."

We started going through my process, working with the staff on their issues. But I did not see the same level of commitment on their part that I typically see when the leaders are actively involved in the process.

In fact, no matter how much reporting I did back to the leaders about who was participating, how well they were taking part, who was blowing off their responsibilities—the leadership essentially did not take the time to support it.

They did not do anything that showed commitment to move that change forward. After working together for 12 weeks or so, we had achieved a few mild successes, but not the change we had hoped for. In the end, they implemented 10 percent or less of what we had worked on, simply because there was no senior-level accountability. Without the leaders being actively involved and watching the dynamics of the group, they were not gaining an understanding of whether they even had the right people and if they did, whether they were being given the right assignments.

Most of the people I worked with in that consulting project are no longer with that company. By failing to communicate commitment to the change process, the leaders cost themselves an investment in training new hires.

My point is if you have strong leadership, and the leadership shows strong direction, then people will come through with the commitment and the follow-through to make change happen.

I do not discount the passion of that CEO and his senior team. The problem was that they (1) just did not communicate that passion in a way that their staff could understand, and (2) they failed to hold people accountable. The result was a culture of disconnects.

The failure in that example might have been as simple as unwillingness on the part of leaders, to make time for staff meetings, and to pull people away from technical work to meet and build cultural common ground together. That is a big issue and I see it in multiple companies. Leaders fail to communicate their passion, and fail to listen to individuals to discover if there is a disconnect on commitment and accountability.

I do not think enough businesses really look at degree of commitment as an obstacle to getting where they want to be. They just assume that everyone is committed to the plan. Too often, in reality, they are not. That lack of commitment can be an obstacle and you may not be aware because people give you lip service, "Yes, we are committed." By now you get my point—without commitment to the direction you are going at every level, you are in for a bumpy ride.

### Balance on the Leadership Team

Does your leadership team have its strengths aligned in a way that is going to allow the organization to grow? You need action-oriented people, who keep pushing for deadlines and results. You need people who are good at connecting with others. But if you had all high-action people, there would be a lot of activity going on and absolutely nothing strategic getting accomplished because they keep moving headlong from one challenge to the next.

You need your social people who keep the group connected, who watch out for the interests of everybody on the team, who create and balance relationships. They will be the optimistic ones, who like to keep everybody happy. But, if you had all social people, it would be all water cooler and no meetings. Productive work would suffer. That is why you need your steady people who just like to keep working away. They support the organization.

You need analytics who will comb through the details and ask tough questions, the people who will say, "Wait a minute. We need to collect some data before we make this decision because we could be going down the wrong path."

## Avoid "Cloning"
**KNOW THIS**

Watch for "cloning." Leaders have a tendency to hire people who possess similar behavioral traits to their own. This may minimize conflict, but it can create serious weaknesses in the organization.

Your leadership team needs to be balanced so you do not have an overwhelming group of action people charging ahead in ten different directions, or too many analytics, making it impossible to act. This is where some behavioral profiling might be useful to help you develop a well-balanced leadership team.

If you do not have a balance of those traits and you do not have them in the right positions, it is going to be very difficult to move a strategy forward. If you are over-weighted in any one area, this can create problems.

This is where leadership comes in as a key element in business growth. People tend to overlook this aspect. The companies that have really been successful in innovating and growing have been very careful about developing a balance of personality traits at the leadership level, creating the culture of the company. They have succession plans and development plans for their key leaders.

**DO THIS**

### Promote from Within or Recruit?

*To fill a leadership position, my bias is toward promoting from within. There is a huge advantage to internal hiring in terms of expertise and morale. However, if the right personality style cannot be found within your ranks, you will want to hire from outside your organization in order to develop a well-balanced leadership team.*

It is easy to change technical skills or learn new technical skills. It is much harder to change attitudes and beliefs.

### Leaders: Don't Be Afraid to Give Up Control

I have worked with companies where leaders are afraid to give too much control to their staff. That can be for a number of reasons.

One common reason is that leaders are confident of their own expertise and doubtful about others' expertise. Maybe these leaders came up through the ranks or they believe for other reasons they know best. Whatever the source of their confidence, these leaders lack the trust to put responsibility in someone else's hands.

Another common reason leaders are afraid to give up control is related to ego and personality. Leaders are individuals involved in their own struggle with their strengths and weaknesses. The good ones will understand what their strengths are and where their weaknesses appear. They will bring people into the team who compensate for those areas where the leader is not strong.

Innovation involves taking risks. One of those risks involves allowing your staff the opportunity to find solutions to the challenges that you face. The staff might come up with a better answer. They might perform functions better than you could do. Some leaders feel that is a threat to their own position within the organization.

Another risk is that someone on staff makes a mistake. Where there's innovation, there is going to be some error because not every experiment is a successful experiment. If you are unwilling to fail, it becomes very challenging to allow your staff to innovate.

I have seen a number of companies that are risk-averse in this way. They do not want to make any mistakes; they do not want to incur those costs.

In one organization I worked with, it was very apparent in their culture that they were out to create the perfect process in which no one could screw up. But if you do that, then people are merely cogs in the machine. They know they need to follow procedures. If they step out of the boundaries of those procedures, they are going to be in error and there could be some disciplinary action taken.

---

**DO THIS**

### Take Managed Risks
*When it comes to taking on risk, it is wise to carefully consider what you stand to gain or lose. Develop a strategy to limit possible negative impacts of the risks you take.*

---

That is where you see a lot of companies struggle. They have very good talent, but that talent just has not been allowed to flourish. Then, when the need for that talent is most critical, they just do not have the ability to step up to the challenge.

### Leaders Lead—Let Staff Do Their Jobs
Your leadership team is going to be weak if they do not know how to work with people to get them serving in the right roles. Too often I have encountered leaders who perceive that the current workforce cannot do a particular task as well they can. Those leaders tend to absorb a lot of work. The result is that the leaders put too much on their plates and do not allow their people to do the work that they were hired to do.

That creates a culture that is not about delegation. It is more about, "I am the supreme being here. I need to make sure this is all done right. And I'm not going to trust somebody else to do the work that I know I can do better." Unfortunately, this type of leader never learns if the staff can do it better or do it differently—he never give them the chance to show their potential.

It is a bigger problem at the frontline and mid-management level, the supportive structure of an organization. A leader who cannot delegate, and get his people aligned to do the right thing, can pull the whole operation apart.

One of the biggest challenges I have seen in companies is promoting people from a very successful worker role into a leadership role without a lot of coaching. They take the widget builder who's really good at what he was doing, and put him in a position of trying to lead a group of people, and develop them into being good widget builders as well. That does not always work. These widget-builders-turned-leaders can be particularly prone to putting too much on their plates. I am not saying you cannot promote from production to leadership—there can be lots of good reasons to do that. It creates a lot of motivation and loyalty in your staff. Your company culture has to include a lot of coaching and support for the individuals who make that transition to leadership.

### Leaders Who Get Stuck in Minutia

A problem related to leaders who take on too much staff work are the leaders who become overburdened dealing with the minutiae of business when they should be focusing on more of the long-term big picture growth. I see this especially at the executive level.

Leadership's responsibility is to be aware of the outside environment and managing risk. Instead they get stuck in the minutiae of day-to-day business. They are doing staff work and managing problems at a level far below what they should be doing given their position in the organization.

That relates back to how well your staff is trained. Have you worked with your staff to make sure that they are doing the work they need to be doing, and that work is not being passed up the chain? Commonly what I see happen is the staff person literally does not understand a situation, or has a problem that he does not know how to fix. He comes to his manager without a solution. The manager says, "Well, I can fix this in five minutes or I can spend an hour teaching these people how to do it."

---

### Coach with Questions, not Answers
*Can your people make a decision without you? Develop their decision-making skills by turning the question around. When someone brings you an issue, ask first, "How do you think we should handle it?" Confirm right solutions and coach the rest.*

DO THIS

---

From a short-term cost-benefit analysis, that five minutes is much easier to digest than the hour or however long it would take to start teaching individuals how to work through the problems. What you do not realize is that with that approach, you actually condition your people to come to you to solve their problems. And that leads to overburdened management dealing with problems that should never have escalated to their level.

If you are training your staff properly, this is what would happen instead. The staff person comes to his manager and says, "Here's the problem we had, here's the solution I came up with, I'm just checking in to make sure it's okay," or, "Here's the solution I implemented, here's the outcome I created, just to keep you aware of what's going on."

Ultimately, I prefer the latter scenario where employees are empowered. They know what they can and cannot do and they know what falls outside of that safe zone and they just handle the problem. They communicate with you what the problem was, how they handled it, and what the outcome was so that you are informed. That is a much more effective organization.

## Staff

Now, let's turn our talent assessment from the leadership's capacity to the staff's. One of the biggest challenges I find when I am working with companies is the tendency to try to make each person into a universal soldier, that worker who can be all things to all people. To do that, you are going to have to take away all their weaknesses. You are going to invest a lot of time and energy in fixing the things that you think are broken about this individual.

Unfortunately, your investment of all that time and energy will achieve only incremental changes in that individual's behavior, usually insignificant changes, because that is not how that person is wired. You cannot take a highly analytical person and turn him into a high-action person if that is not in his nature.

### Balance on the Staff Team

At the beginning of this chapter, I discussed behavioral proofing tools. These tools can help you avoid the "universal soldier" syndrome by allowing you to balance the personalities on the team so they complement each other. A balanced team is capable of more together than any individual would be without the team.

**DO THIS**

### *Can Conflict Be Good?*

*When you have a mix of personality styles on the team there is potential for conflict. Conflict is good—when done right. Make it safe to challenge ideas in your company culture.*

A team needs some analytic types. It needs people who are detail-oriented, think about things, second-guess, and ask questions. But if you have an entire organization full of analytics, it can stall out your company. I have seen a number of companies develop a highly analytical, highly technical staff. They just wallow in the data. They have difficulty trying to innovate, which requires reaching beyond the data on hand.

If you have built a highly analytical culture and you are saying, "We want more innovation," it is going to be very difficult to get there. The analytic types are never going to find enough data to support why you should take that risk.

You need some dominant types on the staff team—people whose higher, deeper selves are high-action. These are the people who will be drivers of innovation. They are very results-oriented. They focus on getting to the finish line. They do not want or need all the details; they just need to know that actions are being taken and results are being produced.

> ### Hire Behaviors, Not Skills                          DO THIS
> *Frankly, I think it is better to hire the right individual from a behavioral aspect and then teach the technical skills needed rather than to hire somebody who is really good on the technical skills and try to develop the right behaviors.*

You need some people-oriented types. They have lots of relationships. They can go into a room, not knowing a single person, and by the time they leave they have made 50 connections. This type is just interested in making sure that everyone is happy and we are all getting along. They are highly optimistic. But they do not necessarily have a lot of drive.

You need some steady types who are persistent and thoughtful. They are somewhere between the analytical and the relationship-driven types, so they are a good connector between the other types. All these personality dynamics play out within the organization.

## Attract and Retain Top Talent

In Jim Collins' book '*Good to Great*' he talks about "who is on the bus right now, and are they in the right seats?" He has got a very good point there. Do you attract talent? What do you do with them?

Consider the example of Lands' End in the 1980s, when getting a job there was a huge deal. New hires had to come in at a lower level, usually part time, and work their way up. It used to be coveted just to get a permanent part-time position there. Lands' End's reputation was that it was a good place to work; partially because of good pay; partially because of a good environment, good benefits, and a corporate culture that really supported the community. They had top talent seeking a job that meant relocating to a rural location an hour away from any good-sized city and starting out part time. That really speaks to the culture they created, the widespread knowledge that Lands' End was a great place to work.

If you have not got that going for you, if you have not got new talent that is actively seeking you out, then the question is, why not? This is about corporate culture. Everything you do with the *Five Tasks of the Golden Apple*, bringing together the strategic aspects of Direction, Path, People, Process, and Measures, is going to create a corporate culture for you that attracts loyal staff (and loyal customers and vendors, too.)

### Keeping Top Talent is Important; So is Turnover

We think of the need for new talent arising out of growth, but the opposite can be true too. When the growth curve has leveled off or started shrinking, often, that is where personnel changes occur. You cut the fat by removing the people who have not been as productive as they should be, and then you try to bring in new talent that can be more productive and get you back in a growth position. The problem is, within the community, the fat-cutting may have created a belief that your company is shrinking or having problems. And most people are not going to seek out a company that is going through financial challenges.

Think about it from the job-seeker's point of view. If you are looking for a new position and you have a choice between a company that you know is experiencing stable growth or is solid and steady at a certain level, versus a company that has just gone through a restructuring and has cut its workforce by 20 percent and is trying to hire a new talent, most people are going to take the safer route. They want to know that they are going to have a paycheck next week and the week after. Plus, no one wants to walk into what is very likely a demoralized workplace.

Attracting top talent is important and keeping them is important too. But any organization needs a certain amount of turnover. All too often people look at just the bad side of turnover. When it is really high, you have a revolving door and people coming in and leaving. That is bad for a number of reasons.

But turnover can prevent problems. If you do not have new blood coming into your organization periodically, you get stalled. While there may be a benefit to having a lot of employees who have been in your company 20, 30 or 40 years, there is also a disadvantage to that. When they are in a place for so long, they become habituated to their routines. People lose the ability to see opportunities or challenges ahead because they are busy in comfortable ruts, focused on their own work.

With the staff you have, and plan to keep, the question becomes, how do you keep them motivated over the long term? That is our challenge as leaders. How do we convince people to do something they would not ordinarily want to do, and do it without us having to negotiate it each time?

The minute you start throwing in monetary incentives, you can create entitlement if you are not careful. Entitlement will crush an organization just as quickly as doing nothing. If the expectation is that, "I am always rewarded for everything I do," where do the rewards stop? When they stop, what happens to motivation? We are all motivated by something. If as leaders we constantly feed that and ramp it up, it is kind of like addiction. An organization I worked with went from, "you get the reward if you get close to this mark," to pushback when we wanted to make small changes without an incentive involved. They would be asking, "What is in it for me?" To be polite, "the JOB'S in it for you." Those are the challenges we run into when we use monetary incentives to create motivation.

Yes, there needs to be motivation, but it does not always have to be something that generates added cost to the organization. Monetary incentives are hard to sustain when the economy goes south and your business model changes. You can no longer provide that incentive, but now there is the expectation, "that is part of my compensation." You see companies go sour on incentives because they see how changes create a negative incentive in the workforce.

Creating a great company culture reduces the need for monetary incentives to keep the staff team motivated. Individuals will be inherently motivated to do the right things, generating the desired outcomes because the environment around them is energizing. They want to be part of making it thrive and grow.

### Managing Staff During Rapid Reduction or Growth

Retaining and motivating staff becomes particularly critical during times of rapid growth or belt-tightening. Most companies in growth mode find that they hire simply because they need bodies to handle the increasing workload. They tend not to look at the efficiency of the operation or the procedures that they have put in place. Their attention is taken up with the challenges of growth. They let go of the culture of incremental improvement—if they had it before the growth spurt, that is. They lose sight of, "we need to constantly look at our process and constantly refine things to make them better."

**DO THIS**

### Interviewing? Ask the Right Questions

*When you are going to be hiring, learn to do behavioral interviewing. In this interview approach, you avoid hypothetical questions. Ask questions based on past history. The applicant's answers will give evidence of personality style better than a hypothetical question will.*

Once you are in growth mode, you plug more people into the equation hoping that it will cover the workload. In the short term it typically does because there is generally more revenue coming in and more work coming in. Any new people you bring in, whether they are well trained or not, typically provide some level of effectiveness in the organization. But are those new individuals working at 60 percent of capacity or are they running at 30 percent capacity?

If you achieve growth at a pace that is almost a vertical slope, it is very difficult to bring people in and train them properly and get them going. Too often the workers are plugged into a position and left to figure it out as they go along. There is a saying that success will kill you faster than failure will. Rapid growth is a terribly difficult thing to manage. It might sound good from the outside, but it is not necessarily something you should hope for in your business. To avoid plugging people into positions without adequate training, develop hiring plans early on, before the need arises. Plan in advance for the circumstances that will require hiring, so you will know when to bring in new staff and know what to assign them to do. When you do hire, select for the right fit in terms of personality.

*KNOW THIS*

***Optimize Current Staff Before Hiring More***
*Rapid hiring can lead to wasteful spending. Optimize people to get to 80 percent productive capacity before adding more staff.*

I would counsel you to avoid using a behavioral profiling tool to determine if a particular individual is somebody you should hire. I think the proper role for assessments is to help you understand the behaviors, motivations, and attitudes you are going to encounter, if you hire a particular individual, which is a different conversation from the "go or no go" decision. My perspective is that behavioral profiling should focus on how to work with the people you hire to bring out their full potential.

## Getting ROI from Training and Development

I honestly believe that most companies see the value in training and development. They realize they should make training part of the business plan. I also know that when economic shifts start to happen, training is usually the first thing that gets the axe. Leaders see the value in it, but short-term they feel they just cannot afford it, and for now it is something they believe they can cut without negative results. The problem is they have never made that value tangible. They have never shown how training and development produces an ROI. They tend to say, "The easiest way we can save money is by cutting back on any sort of training or development of our people, because cutting that delivers an immediate return to the bottom line in the short-term."

At one of my past jobs, I remember going to a day-long seminar with six or eight of my co-workers. There were motivational speakers who provided a lot of good information. But it became clear they were there to sell their books, or get us to buy into their consulting, or whatever. We brought back a lot of material, which we tried to implement. The entire rest of the staff looked at us as if we had grown two heads. They had not been through that seminar experience. They had no connection. We just could not get their buy-in. Not only did our ideas fall on deaf ears, but we were ridiculed about it. "Okay, if that's the way this will be treated, what's the point?" Investment was made in our time and travel, and we came back with enthusiasm to use what we had learned, but we got nowhere.

If that is the type of training you do, then I would say go ahead, cut back, because the material you are getting, although it may be good, is not being used anyway. Therefore, why make the investment if you are not going to retain the value?

The reason training and development is first to be cut is that most people perceive it as non-measurable. They know there is value in it somewhere, but they cannot tie it to bottom-line dollars. You do gain from training if you do it right. If it is aligned with your vision, there is a purpose behind it, there is some direction, and accountability afterward, and it is engrained within the culture, then it sticks. If you are doing it as a feel-good thing or because others say you need to, you are not going to get the same results.

## Employee Development Plans: Who Decides Who Learns What?

Many leaders believe that employees should be able to figure out what they need to develop themselves. But do people really

> ### *Employee Development is a Team Effort*
> *Planning for individual development is a team effort that should include both the employee and his or her manager. Team leaders need to understand employees' goals and how their strengths apply to where they want to go. Establish tangible measures to monitor whether development is meeting the expectations of both the individual and the team.*

**KNOW THIS**

choose the training you, as the leader, see as the best next strategic move for them? I know lots of people for whom training is either a free day out of the office or a mini-vacation. They will propose a 3- or 4-day retreat at a nice location, and at a time when they want to get away. Yes, it does make sense to send people where they can disengage from day-to-day work to engage with the training. And recreation should be factored in. But how does it tie into your culture? How do you hold them accountable in such a way that when those people come back, they bring new ideas, and they are given a chance to apply those ideas in a positive way?

You also have to look at individual learning styles. Not everyone learns the same way. Saying "Everyone's going to go to the same retreat, and this is how we're all going to work," does not cut it. The training and development you need in your business plan requires a more customized, strategic view than that.

I do not see enough involvement by senior leadership on what

> ### *Use Training for Reinforcement*
> *Training works well with individuals who are already doing the right things. The information they receive in the training will reinforce the established behavior.*

**DO THIS**

that training and development should be. In too many organizations, people are allowed, and even encouraged, to choose for themselves. There might be some initial value to that, but there are not any long-term outcomes for the company as a result of it.

It comes down to focusing on making sure that there is a clear vision, and that training experiences align clearly with the vision of a company. It must also align with the direction of individuals, who should have a career path they are working towards and that is discussed openly at regular intervals with their leader.

For training and development to be effective, it has got to result in change, real change. You have got to set up the situation to sustain that learning, so when those individuals return to the office they do not fall back into the same old habits and nothing changes.

### Culture Changes When You Cut Training and Development

When you cannot associate something with a positive outcome other than a "feel good" emotion, it just makes sense to cut it. However, there are several impacts that go with doing that. People notice when you quit investing in your organization, and it starts changing the dynamics of your culture. The moment you start reducing and cutting back, your people start holding back because if their minds are not stimulated, they get focused on the same minutiae you are focused on. They worry about why the company is not growing, and what is going to happen to their job. Instead of worrying about the problem they could be working on it with the right training and development.

So many of the programs out there are quick, relatively inexpensive, sound good, give you a lot of good information, but produce virtually zero results. That just drives me insane. Most training experiences are not set up in a way that allows the individual to retain a lot of information.

Low-cost classes that are a half-day or a couple of hours, or a full day or maybe a weekend, typically do little to produce positive outcomes. A longer process is needed to incorporate the training, so that these new concepts can start becoming habits.

It is very difficult to throw ten tons of information on an individual and expect them to retain it all and then process it, and more importantly, execute it, so somehow the training has to be broken down in a way that is digestible. People are able to incrementally start doing these things and making the changes at a micro-scale in the beginning, leading to significant improvements over time.

There are two areas in which I feel training can have significant benefit for an organization, and they are tightly related. I believe in improving teamwork skills, and developing the team's ability to have productive meetings. When a work group has these skills in place, it improves its capacity to innovate, solve problems, and work effectively.

### How to Form Teams

I have done a lot of training with my clients on how to improve capacity for teamwork. One exercise stands out in my memory.

I developed a process where I took a large group of people through an exercise on team building. The secret that I did not tell anyone in the group, was that the point of the exercise was to expose the dysfunctions of a team.

My co-facilitators and I had a room filled with a bunch of egos that all believed they knew how to manage teams better than anyone else. There were about 80 people in the room. I gave them interlocking puzzle pieces in about 20 different colors. They had to match up the colors to find their teammates. I did not tell them any reasoning behind it. This forced different people to come together, with no definition of who these people were, or how they were going to fit the team.

From there, I took them through a questioning exercise—what are the typical challenges most people have in their business.

I had them throw out a bunch of answers, which included topics like increased sales, getting the marketing message right, and managing the sales funnel. I then gave each group a challenge from the list to work on. I said, "You have the next 30 minutes to come up with what might be the best possible solution." And then I just sat back.

I saw each of the groups just look at each other. Some people would jump into it. Other people would be confused and some people would get frustrated because they did not know what was going on. They did not know what they should be doing.

Through the organics of it, basically everyone came around to the realization that this is what most teams go through. The exercise just accelerated the process because we narrowed the timeline and we threw everyone together in a group, but there was no discussion.

That is when I concluded the exercise and said, "Okay, now let's talk about what makes a successful team." We got into each person figuring out how they interacted with the team, what their responsibility was within the team, what their specific outcomes were.

The takeaway from this exercise is that most teams are just thrown together based more on their technical abilities than how they are supposed to interact and what sort of outcomes they are supposed to create. There is no training or process on how to work together to be the most effective group possible.

They are not taught that it is good to have push back, it is good to have disagreements and discussions, and get people involved and passionate. At the same time, there needs to be respect for everyone on the team and inclusion of everyone on the team to make it work. Training exercises that bring out these lessons, through experiences, are worth investing in.

### Participate Productively in Meetings

I am not a fan of more meetings. I am a fan of productive meetings. Most meetings get tied up in the minutiae of day-to-day work, which really should be handled other ways. I find that many meetings take place but end with very little productive output. I think back to some of my work experiences. There was one organization I worked with, in particular, where we scheduled meetings to have meetings, to schedule more meetings, to have more meetings. There just never was any production that came through those meetings. In fact, many of the things that we specifically discussed at a meeting were left to be dealt with at another point because nobody would decide on it. It was a bit of a passive-aggressive culture, where people felt, "I don't want to upset anyone else so we're just not going to make a decision now. We'll talk about it behind the scenes and then, hopefully, we'll come back to it in a week." But so many times, we never did bring closure to an agenda item because we were all stuck in a culture that avoided tough conversation or decisions that might pit people against each other.

---

### Respect the Owners

*Recognize who "owns" the proposed solutions that come forward in meetings. Make sure those who originally proposed a solution remain involved in exploring its potential application. If the idea is implemented, make sure the original "owner" knows and takes pride in that.*

DO THIS

---

There are ways to have difficult conversations that do not involve attacking egos and do not involve challenging somebody's ideas. There are positive ways to challenge people that spur them to produce something greater, and there are negative ways that just shut people down and make them not want to contribute. To stimulate positive conversations, keep people solution-focused. What is going well; what will make things better? This creates a better climate for discussion than focusing on what is wrong and needs fixing. Encourage solutions to come from staff, as well as the research to discover how their proposed solutions will work.

This ties back to strong leadership. Your organization needs leaders who can conduct meetings that are effective, that have real outcomes. You need leaders who challenge ideas without shutting down contributions. This aspect of leadership is about creating a company culture where people work together effectively. One of the best things you could do for your company is to bring in the training and development that creates a culture of productive meetings.

## To Be a Golden Apple Company, Embrace Change

In Chapter 3, I defined Golden Apple companies as recognized industry leaders who can charge a premium price, well above the thick part of the bell curve of pricing where most of their competitors compete. What makes a curve-breaking company is their commitment to change. They manage risk, accept being uncomfortable, and stay at the leading edge, where they can get that premium price, simply through embracing change.

The leaders in these companies understand that change is the only constant. They embrace change, but not just for change's sake. They recognize that change is an ongoing part of the process of growth and innovation.

Many leaders want to get processes in place and then not worry about them. They want to know that the process that works today is going to work tomorrow and hopefully work ten years from now. They are prone to get stuck in ruts, out of a failure of willingness to accept change, because change is difficult and uncomfortable.

You need to make change a consistent feature of your organization, but make it change that is positive, well understood, well explained, and executed with significant buy-in throughout the organization.

Your staff needs to be clear about why this change needs to happen. Most importantly, they need to see the leadership working through the change process, committed and accountable at every step.

Experiencing a change process is like riding a rollercoaster. There are going to be highs and lows while the change becomes the new "normal." In the beginning there is a certain degree of high euphoria that might come out of a change process because, if you realize how it is going to benefit you, you might be excited about making that change happen.

However, when you get headlong into making that change happen, you start running against the roadblocks and the obstacles. Now you are pushed back on your new beliefs.

It is like taking up exercise. There might be a lot of excitement in the beginning about your new workout. Then after a few days you start getting the aches and pains and the soreness, and you are tired of sweating, and you think about how you could be doing other things—your mind wants to push you back to where you were before.

> ### *Lead the Charge Up the Learning Curve*
> *Most people quit before they give themselves a chance to succeed. As a leader, get your people to understand that the point at which they are feeling the greatest frustration with a change is actually when they should continue pushing on. The trigger behavior: When people start complaining that the old way is much better than the new one, break down where the challenges are taking place. Often it is part of the normal learning curve.*

This is where you get to the low point of that rollercoaster, where you are moving away from what you were familiar with into something that is completely new, and now you are feeling the resistance. Typically the resistance gets strongest when you are at your lowest point. That is when people tend to revert back to their old habits. They give up on the change process because they have lost their sense of direction about why that change is necessary.

It is the responsibility of leadership to stay committed to the process and to realize when people are hitting that low point. That's the time when you, as a leader, need to push harder on making change happen. You have got to work through those low points of the rollercoaster so that the staff can get back to focusing on the change their making.

I see a lot of leaders fail when they encounter so much push-back and resistance from the staff that they become convinced the change process is not working. I have seen this process go on for years. I can think of companies that I have worked for that were trying to make significant changes to their process, and their staff was having nothing to do with it. They were even going as far as sabotaging certain things to show that it would not work. There was little to no buy-in at the staff level. The leaders had already stacked the cards against themselves on that change process by failing to get their staff's buy-in. As a result, it became a battle of wills. It takes leadership to get through that situation. At that low point on the rollercoaster, leaders need to come in with the sustained message, "Keep at it, this is working."

### Managing the Risks in Change

One of the biggest risks in change is the natural fear we have of the possible negative outcomes. This is the fear that causes us to undermine or avoid change, to stay in the relative safety of "the way we do things now." Yes, it is possible to do the wrong thing. But in most cases, the terrible scenario we imagine is never the scenario that actually happens. The acronym for fear is "False Emotion Appearing Real". Humans tend to be negatively wired. We are apt to focus on that worst-case scenario, believing negative statements like, "If we do this and we get it wrong, we'll go bankrupt within three years." That is a reality, but one that can be managed.

If you accept the possibility that negative outcomes can happen, you should be able to put contingencies in place to protect yourself from those scenarios.

Other risks related to change are the demands for resources in terms of money, time and talent.

Money is always at risk because change nearly always requires investment. How do you manage that investment to make sure you get the most out of it? Leaders need to be cognizant of what they are spending money on, who is going to do it, what the timeline for the payments is, and what results are expected of the investment. Who is going to manage those results and how is the process going to roll out? Leaders need to use accountability to manage the risk in spending money.

Time is at risk. There may be training in new processes required or downtime while mechanical systems are re-engineered. Timelines need to be coordinated so what is needed is in place when and where it should be. Business moves at high speed these days and the risks in getting timing wrong must be managed.

And finally, your people are a source of risk. If you do not have a strong culture, will your people support the necessary change and make it happen? The biggest mistake a leadership team could make is not addressing the attitudes people bring to the change and getting people to work through their fears. If instead you let the problems fester to a point where you are absolutely forced to confront them, you will be doing it with reduced time, money, and resources.

### Make Change "Business as Usual"

Your company culture needs to make change the norm. Everybody needs to get comfortable with being uncomfortable. It is our nature to be risk-averse, to desire comfort and safety. Once we have achieved comfort and safety we want to preserve them. It is much easier to avoid conflict and avoid taking certain actions because you know you will create a level of discomfort in people, departments, and the entire organization, whatever it might be.

Change does not successfully happen without people getting a little uncomfortable. Now, there is an acceptable level of discomfort and there is an unacceptable level. We need to manage that comfort zone in a way that encourages people to make change happen and help them understand that their feelings of uncertainty are actually okay because that is what gets the creative gears turning.

Unfortunately, we have very short memories and because of our nature of wanting to be in our comfort zones, we tend to put off problems that are small today only to deal with them when they are bigger and out of control problems in the future. I have worked with a number of companies that were aware of certain problems within the organization, but failed to deal with them at the appropriate time because the pain was not great enough. They knew it was a problem, but they were still making good money, and things were still going well enough. They did not see the need to invest at the time.

Then when the economy shifted, or when regulations changed, all of a sudden these problems were blown to the forefront. And now they must be addressed immediately. There is a greater cost to addressing them because now it has become an emergency situation.

And there is a greater risk that you will not be successful because time, money, and resources are in tighter supply. You have less ability to manage that situation and make that change. You have lost a lot of opportunity.

## People: Impact on Customers

When you get the third task of a Golden Apple company right, the impact on your customers is huge. You will be visible in the marketplace, because loyal customers will be talking about you. They will be conveying the message that you may not be the cheap-

**KNOW THIS**

### Exercise Your Creativity
*Creativity is like a muscle. It requires exercise to be effective. Find ways to build creativity into everyone's work.*

est option, but you provide the greatest value, the highest level of ROI for what you do. When your name is mentioned everyone is going, "Yes, they are the best in the business."

Companies do not look at reputation hard enough. Probably the biggest differentiator for most companies is the reputation they create. Do not be afraid to survey your customers, to find out if you are achieving that positive visibility. I find a number of business leaders are cautious about approaching clients for evaluation, because they do not want to hear bad news. That is a mistake. It is important to go to your clients and ask for some honest feedback.

**DO THIS**

### Use the Net Promoter Score Metric
*The Net Promoter Score is a way of looking at how your customers judge you, by asking one question: "How likely are you to you recommend this company to a friend or colleague?" The response score functions as a metric for reputation.*

If you want to know how you are doing with the "people" aspect of your business, just ask your customers. They are the ones receiving the experience your people deliver. The secret to building true competitive differentiation into your company rests with your people.

**Chapter**

# 7

# The Fourth Task of the Golden Apple: Process

To become a Golden Apple company, pay attention to processes. Every business needs processes in place for standardization. This may sound simple, but it's really quite a challenge. As a business grows and adds staff, it's very easy to become inconsistent with the product or service you deliver if you do not have a process in place. One person might do the work one way while another person might do it completely differently. If there is not any alignment on production process, there is a potential to create problems.

On the other side of the coin, if you become too rigid within your processes, people become totally dependent on the process. You take away their ability to innovate. The balance between standardization and flexibility is delicate for any business. It becomes particularly challenging when the business must operate in a highly regulated environment. Banks are a good example, but I can think of a number of different industries where finding a workable balance between uniformity and flexibility is a challenge.

> **Process Creates Consistency**
> *Process is a template for producing consistent results. But business demands innovation, so processes become obsolete. Every process should be evaluated and challenged constantly.*

**KNOW THIS**

Companies that operate with very low tolerance for risk and a high level of regulation find that very strict guidelines about standardized work processes are necessary. The problem is, when an issue comes up that does not fit a specified process, people must develop a workaround. Believe it or not, your employees can get crafty with what their workarounds might be. If they do not understand why the process is in place or do not understand the vision or the values of the company, they may come up with a workaround that produces the wrong result. That's why it is important to make sure people understand not only the process itself, but all the "hows and whys" around it.

It is equally important to have a clear understanding of the outcomes that need to be created to align with the direction of the company. Every process has to support the vision, mission, and values—it has to function within the guidelines that keep you on the path toward your destination.

In a company culture where that understanding does not exist, people are likely to step outside those parameters. For example, a person might come up with a workaround that he believes is in the best interest of the company and of the customer or client, yet that workaround could be very costly. In a highly regulated industry (as with financial institutions) the wrong workaround could lead to falling out of compliance, which could result in fines and even government involvement.

### Too Much Flexibility Creates Problems

If we look at the banking crises of 2008, 2009 and 2010, one of the biggest challenges within the banking industry is related to compliance and leadership. The leaders did not put value on compliance. They encouraged a kind of creativity that led outside the guidelines for operation of financial institutions.

Banking industry regulators generally look at a certain set of variables, but the crises have led to an increased focus on one specific variable from that set; management. The failure of certain leaders has led directly to this greater scrutiny. Examiners are looking at how well management understands the direction in which they are taking the bank; how well management understands the challenges they are facing; how well management is working with their board of directors to make decisions about solutions to those challenges. Examiners want to be sure that if there is a problem, management has a solution—they have figured out how they are going to dig themselves back out of the hole that they are currently in, no matter how shallow or deep that hole may be.

As the banking crises shows, you need an understanding not just of outcomes, but of parameters that must be met in the process. Allow too much flexibility or creativity in the process, or having a process that is inadequate, resulting in workarounds that will lead to trouble unless you have created a company culture where all people understand the vision, mission, and values, and are able to follow, or when necessary, create processes that support that direction.

### Too Much Standardization Creates Problems, Too

If you rely on complete standardization to avoid the problems of flexibility, you really have not protected yourself. Your company could reach a point where you have become so dependent on process that you have taken away the potential for innovation. People's brains shut down when they are required to just follow the steps and follow them blindly.

Typically I see this happens where there is a rigid structure in place and the leadership team has instructed their staff not to deviate from that structure. The people just follow the process and then when something comes up that is not within that process, they are unable to propose any answer beyond, "That's our policy. That's the way we do things." Those are words customers do not like to hear!

### The Need for Cultural Alignment

When the people in your company are aligned with the overall direction and path of the company, they tend to find the right balance between flexibility and standardization of processes. When they see a possibility for process improvement they will bring their innovative ideas to the table.

When people are not in alignment with your company culture, two things might happen. Either they will just shut down and follow the specified processes to the nth degree, or they will find a workaround, which becomes an unwritten process that you are unaware of. This could create further problems down the road. Suppose the workaround impacts how the customer experiences your company. What if the person who is following that unwritten process moves on and is no longer with the organization. The worker who replaces that person will not know that unwritten workaround, which the customer has come to expect, and that creates an upset customer.

**DO THIS**

### *Communicate Company Values Consistently*
*To keep processes consistent, keep communicating about your company's values. A shared understanding of the company's value set helps guard against the workarounds people might otherwise come up with.*

As a leader, you have the opportunity to create a valuable point of competitive differentiation by creating a culture where processes exist, but they are not so standardized as to be unreasonably inflexible or inclined to inhibit innovation in your people, nor are they so flexible that they lead to failures in compliance or quality of the outcome.

## Assessing the Process

Leaders should hold themselves accountable for assessing their own processes, and they should establish that expectation with the people they lead. So often, a process is created and then it is never touched again. In part that is because we are creatures of habit. We do not like change and if we can put something in place permanently, that keeps us in our comfort zones. If change needs to happen, we only discover that fact as a reactionary measure. In too many companies, the leaders are not constantly looking at processes for continual opportunities to improve and update. As a leader you should always be asking the question, especially when you start running into roadblocks or challenges, "Is this process the best way to do this or is there a way we can do it better?"

When people start a job with a new company, it is not uncommon to have insights into the processes that might have escaped the people who have been there for years. During the first three months, the new hire sees everything that everyone else who has been in that company for years has been doing. Any newcomer might end up just scratching his or her head and saying, "I wonder why they do it this way? This does not make any sense."

I have encountered companies that have long since evolved away from a particular reporting tool or data set, yet they continue to produce reports. They are tracking information that is no longer relevant. And I have seen companies that are taking ten steps to complete a process that could be done in three, if they took the time to examine the process. The leaders in these companies are not holding themselves or others accountable for process assessment.

I have seen people come into a new organization with a new idea for a process, and be immediately squashed. The newcomers are not given any reason why no one is taking action on the new process idea. In some cases, there might be a valid reason why this particular idea will not work. But the newcomers are not given the reason. Here is a chance to open up dialog. This is an opportunity to model the process of thinking through an innovative idea. "Well, if

> ### *Outside Looking In*
> *Outsiders can often find problems in a process quicker than people who have been doing the process for years. Within the first month that a new hire is with you, ask for his or her perspective on your processes. This could be part of the training and development of new hires or a personal welcome from the leaders. Just ask what they see that works, what they see that does not work, and what questions they have about the processes they have encountered.*

**DO THIS**

we were to do it that way, what other challenges or obstacles will we face? What are some possible solutions to that?" And so on.

If you encourage newcomers to research their proposed ideas, they find where the obstacles are. If you tell them, it just shuts them down. Those people are less likely to come forward with new ideas. I see this time and time again and I even hear leaders complain about how their people do not bring fresh ideas.

When the leaders ask their staff for feedback on a particular process they just will not share their thoughts. Or if they do, they will add, "Well, you guys are not going to do anything about it anyway." And here is why—the leaders have created a culture where people shut down because they do not feel like they are being validated. Their suggestions get ignored or sidelined without explanation.

That is why it's so important to engage in a conversation and keep the ownership with the individuals who brought the ideas. You will experience continual process improvement when you have them work through the proposed change, identify the obstacles, figure out what the workarounds would be, and find the possible solutions.

### Visualize the Process

I was contracted to consult with a manufacturing company about their bidding process. We looked at the steps from the first bids all the way to getting those bids to production. We found that their process called for information to be passed two, three, even four times between several different departments. We were able to redesign the process as more of a straight-line pass.

There were too many touches in the system, which was creating problems. It was eating up a lot of time, and it was causing confusion. The customer never saw this, and the employees involved really did not think anything of it, because that's the way they had always done it. The process worked, but it was not efficient.

As their consultant, I sat down with them and we talked through the process in detail, step, by step, by step. We then flow-charted the process. We visualized how the information moved through the organization. When you can visualize a process, you can see all the decision points.

My client realized how many different decision points were part of the process. The way they were handling those decision points was causing a lot of momentum wasted in moving things around. By visualizing the process they could see redundancies, where information was brought to a certain point, and then looped back up to the starting point, only to be brought back through the system again. When that happens, two or three times in a process, that is usually a sign of a problem. Once we could visualize how information was moving and where it was going, it became very apparent where time was being wasted.

---

### Use Tools to Make Process Mapping Simple

*Tools exist to make mapping out a process simple. Mind-mapping and flow-charting software are two such tools. You will find more about techniques for mapping processes later in this chapter.*

DO THIS

---

I worked with a banking client on visualizing their processes. For them it was a compliance issue, because they needed to know how information was moving through their systems. They needed documentation of how loans were being handled, because if loans were not handled in a very consistent manner—certain points were not covered in great detail with their clients and certain information was not collected internally—it could have lead to fines or worse. Unfortunately for this client, process improvement did not involve making the process any easier or more efficient. It was more about avoiding future pain caused by not having an adequate process in place. The client actually had to put more steps into the system, to stay in compliance with regulations and laws affecting the banking industry.

## *How Process Relates to Goals*

Throughout this book, I have invited you to set your sights on a destination for your business—a Direction. We have looked at how your Path and your People should align to carry you toward that destination. Like those components of your business, Process can carry you toward your goals—if you design your processes well, and continually examine them to be sure that, as other aspects of your business evolve, your processes stay in sync with those evolving needs.

The three factors to consider about your business processes are:

- Does this process make you competitive?
- Can you profit from this process?
- Is this process as efficient as possible?

First, let's look at process from the aspect of competition. This affects your price point. Maybe you have processes in place that are serving you well enough, but competitors are crushing you on price or quality. As I said in Chapter 3 on the Pitfalls of Price Differentiation, you should not set out to have the cheapest offering—in some cases, you might even want to be the most expensive. You still have to look at what you are doing and be sure your margins put you in a good position to meet or beat your competition.

Next, let's look at the profit piece. Ask—"Can we grow from this process? Is it going to be business-sustainable? Are we innovative? Are we looking into the future and seeing how we can constantly evolve our processes to keep them above industry standards? "

Finally, consider efficiency. Every company needs to look at ways it can become more efficient. If you do that continually, not just when the market is slow, it is going to help your business when you do have downturns because you are already engaged in planning for efficiency.

We tend to get sloppy when the money is rolling in, and because we have very short memories and quickly forget how we operated when things were bad. Really, you always need to be thinking about how you can make your business more efficient. You should always be investing in that level of innovation where you keep your processes tight; you hire people when they are needed and when they can be most productive; not just when they are filling gaps because you are growing so fast, you just need to throw a body in there to try and get more work done. That is where companies get in trouble.

Typically, when most companies looking at processes, management focuses on how they can get from point A to point B the quickest without negatively impacting the customer, or at least minimizing any negative impacts. Typically we want to streamline as much as possible. There are several reasons:

- When we have fewer decision points, the likelihood a mistake will be made becomes smaller.
- When we take less time getting from point A to point B, less manpower is needed for the process.
- A more streamlined process can translate to quicker delivery times to the customer. Quicker delivery times mean quicker accounts receivable time—you get paid faster.

So, typically, in most organizations, leaders look at processes asking, "How can I be more efficient to cut down on my labor cost? How can I be more efficient to get paid quicker? How can I be more profitable? If I have to be competitive in certain areas, how I can do it?"

All these factors—competitiveness, profit potential, efficiency—come into play when you examine our processes. Improving on any of these aspects, or all of them, is good for the organization.

## Customer Impact: Creating Loyalty

Process does not just involve the systems to handle products or to move information through a company. There is also a process related to creating customer loyalty.

This involves looking at the customer experience. You can take your process and essentially lay over the top of it the customers' view. What is the customer experience going to be related to this process?

When customers walk into your business, what do they see? How do they react? How are they treated? How should they be treated? What is the outcome you are looking to create for the customer? How can you make it a very positive experience for them?

There are several different touch points within an organization where your customers interact. And it is more than just walking through your door or navigating around your website. Today, they are finding information through messages that were not shaped and distributed by you. Social networking hubs like Twitter and Facebook carry conversations about your company. Plus, people are visiting different sites that allow them to rank and critique businesses. You have a lot more to manage now than ever in terms of the impact of processes on customers. Failure to "get it right" will be more public.

**KNOW THIS**

### *Consistency Creates Trust*

*Is yours a company that customers can count on? Buyers want to know what to expect before building trust in the outcome. Your customers will keep coming back—if you deliver a consistent experience.*

Unfortunately, in many cases process work tends to be reactionary. The leaders do not worry about the customer experience because they assume that they are doing a great job, or at least giving the same degree of customer service that competitors do. But that is another of the pitfalls I pointed out in Chapter 3—getting stuck in "me too," allowing your competitors to set your business strategies. If your customer service is about the same as the others out there, you are not leveraging it as a differentiator.

That is why it is so important to look at the customer service experience and look at the process that goes on to support it. Consider how you take care of that customer from beginning to end. Can you find a way to do it better? Now you are using your processes to gain an edge in competitive differentiation.

I have been working with an accounting firm to solve a client service issue. Talking with them, I discovered one of their biggest challenges was having correct contact information on file. People who had face-to-face contact with clients were failing to ask if there had been any changes to the contact information. We set about designing a process improvement to make sure that 90 percent of the information gathered in their database is accurate. Clients move, they change email addresses, they change phone numbers.

It is not usually top-of-mind for the client to contact everybody and say, "Oh, by the way, I have a new phone number." Or "I have a new email address now." This accounting firm needed a process that would trigger the staff to get that information. We came up with a simple solution. First, we made changes to a few fields in their database to indicate when information was last updated. Second, we made it part of the process that whenever staff are talking to a client, they are looking at this database to see when information was last updated. They are reminded to ask the client if there have been any changes in contact information. The third step is going into the database, putting initials and the date when information is updated, so that people can see when information was last checked, and by whom. With this system you are not bothering the client by asking them every time you talk, has anything changed? That was one of the firm's big concerns. Now they can see how much time has passed, and if it has been six months or more since that contact information was last checked, they know to inquire about any changes. That is a process that not only streamlines a function for the office, because they do not have to go chasing down inaccurate information, but also making it easier for the client as well.

## Techniques for Mapping Processes

Mapping out your processes does not need to be a big chore. You just need a way to show information about how a process passes through your organization, for example how a product gets from raw materials through assembly and out to the customer. You can do the same thing with customer service, mapping how a customer is handled throughout the sales process. There are standard techniques for this.

It is as simple as getting a basic flow chart software program. I think everyone in management should get a basic understanding of flow charts, using the symbols for decision points, processes, documents, and so on. I don't think you have to go into it to the nth detail; a basic knowledge is important, and easy to get. That said, I believe there is a place for having an outside consultant walk through mapping your processes with you. That outside person is going to ask questions and not make the assumptions that typically happen inside an organization.

I have found with my clients that by walking through a process together, looking at every step, we are able to identify where they might have rolled five steps into one. With my fresh eyes I see what they have overlooked. There could be six steps going on between one step and another that they have just made the assumption everyone knows, and thus skipped over.

**DO THIS**

## *Hunt Down the Redundancies*

*When you break down a process into its component steps, look for where there are loops in the process. Often we repeat steps as a failsafe. How can you find and eliminate those redundancies to create a more efficient flow in the process?*

It is important to break a process down to every step involving a decision. What decision is being made? Does it depend on previous decisions, and does that decision lead to another decision? Pretty soon what my client saw as "steps one and two" expanded into 20 or 30 different steps to be covered. Mapping the process brings this additional complexity to light. That's when you really start to see, "Oh, my gosh! This is really all the stuff we have to go through just to move a customer or a process along." It puts you in a good position to see where a process could be streamlined or where innovation could make you stand out from the competition.

If for example, you were a retail establishment, for example a bookstore or small restaurant, you could take "visualizing" literally—actually take pictures of the environment. Looking at the flow that happens, especially in restaurants, can reveal opportunities for process improvement. You will see how the layout is functioning, from the grill area to the front counter, to the wait stations, to the seating. Watch how your workers flow between your customers, the kitchen, back and forth. This allows you to see where bottlenecks occur. It also gives you a better understanding of what the customer is seeing in your retail business.

In retail you are highly visible to your customers. They can see when you are doing things really well. And they can see when you are inefficient. Visualizing processes, using techniques like flow charts or photos, gets people to stop, take a look, and say, "What's wrong here? What do we need to change? How can we make this better?"

### Process Mapping Leads to Innovation

Visualizing what you are doing, by mapping the process, will drive innovation.

There is an old story heard in marketing circles about the hardware store that conducted research into customer behavior by putting a bucket of peanuts next to the front door. Watching where the peanut shells ended up on the floor told the hardware store owner volumes about how traffic flowed through the store, and where people paused and focused their attention. That is a very low-tech form of process mapping. I do not recommend that technique because somebody's going to slip on a peanut shell. We have better technology. Most places use some sort of point-of-sale software that can produce similar data.

A retailer could use point-of-sale software to find ways to innovate on product line strategies by tracking what people are buying.

Look at what are your top-selling items. Correlate your point-of-sale data to your product displays. There are some companies that put high-demand items in specific spots to create traffic through their store, like putting the milk at the back of a grocery. The advantage to the retailer is that the customer is going to walk past a lot of other items and there will be impulse buys. The customer will walk out with a half dozen other purchases in addition to what they came in for. Of course, you can upset your customers with that strategy if your store is large. It's just a matter of how you balance the two. The retailer has to make a profit. Their margins are such that they are making pennies on items. The innovation here could be displaying items by usage groups. If people are running in to pick up milk, display cereal near it. Display things that you use together. Looking at your point of sale data would really help you see what people buy together, so you can develop usage groups in your display strategy.

**KNOW THIS**

### Compete Where Others Are Not

*Where is your competition weakest? How could you use an innovation in your processes to take advantage of their weaknesses?*

Most companies talk about innovation, but few actually act, because with innovation comes risk. The greater the innovation, the higher the degree of risk involved. Most organizations do not want to manage that risk, because it could put their company in jeopardy, depending on how big that risk might be. If you can find a way to innovate through process improvement, streamlining for efficiency for example, or adding more opportunities for customer engagement, you have got a meaningful point of competitive differentiation that can allow you to leap past competitors.

## Innovation in Process

As I said at the opening of this chapter, every business needs effective processes in place, with enough flexibility to allow for innovation, but enough standardization that they give customers a consistent experience and encourage staff alignment with your overall culture. So what can you do to get your processes where they need to be?

Get people to start asking the "why" questions about your processes. "Why are we doing things this particular way? Is this the best way?" From there, the next step is to visualize what is going on. Map the process. Break it down. If you discover a workaround, does it fall within the parameters of your company culture? Does it meet your vision? Your value set? If that workaround helps you stay on the right path, headed in the right direction then it needs to be formalized as process. If not, you need to solve the issue that led to that workaround.

This is a process that repeats over time in your business. You should be working within continuums, not events. If process analysis is continually going on, it will not take days to complete. Once you start doing it on a regular basis, you will soon reach a point where you are tweaking what is already working, making it more efficient. Process becomes a 10 or 15-minute conversation, every so often, as opposed to every two years discovering your process needs a major overhaul. That involves pulling very expensive people into an office, working all this stuff out, getting to where you know what the new processes need to be—and now you have change management issues with implementation because you have let too much time go by without examining your processes.

Remember, the goal here is incremental, not monumental (and therefore disruptive) change.

---

**Five "Why's"**                                                  DO THIS

*An instructor once told me the best way to get to the root of a problem is to ask "why"—and keep asking it a total of five times. Each "why" digs deeper into the previous answer until fundamental insights come to light.*

153

## Chapter

# 8

# The Fifth Task of the Golden Apple: Measures

Many a consultant will tell you organizational development is measurable, but few will tell you how. I am not going to be able to tell you exactly how to measure your organization, either, because that is entirely unique to each company. I will, however, give you a framework for understanding what to measure, and how, in order to make your company a high-performing, highly-differentiated Golden Apple.

The highway analogy has kept turning up in every aspect of the Golden Apple Company that I have discussed. Stretching that analogy a little further, it is time to get behind the wheel and figure out what gauges are on the instrument panel, and what they can tell you about your direction, your speed of travel, your fuel level. It is time to pop open the hood and see exactly what evidence is available about how this vehicle is running. Measures are the indicators you need to tell if your company is on the right Path, headed toward your chosen Direction.

In many cases, this means discovering ways to take factors that are intangible, and therefore difficult to measure, and finding a relationship with a tangible factor that can be measured.

For example, a lot of companies talk about wanting better communication or improved customer service. Well, that sounds good. You can envision what better communication or improved customer service would look like. But how do you know when you actually achieve them? How do you know when you get better communication, for example? And what will better communication do for you?

What would be a measure of better communication? I will give you an example.

I worked with a company where the leader wanted better communication within his manufacturing company and within his leadership team.

We dug into it. The reason there was a need for the better communication was that there was a lot of work stoppage. Many people were asking questions, unsure about what to do when. They completed one project but were not sure how or when to move on to the next project. We were able to make the association between communication and the work stoppages. Our measure became, "We will know we have better communication when we can eliminate downtime."

**DO THIS**

### *Make Measures Relevant to the Group*

*In today's business world we are inundated with data. Different data sets are relevant to different groups. Parse down the data available so that people only get data that is relevant to their roles. This will help avoid "data paralysis."*

The analysis started with the desired end result, then worked backwards. We went through every process to figure out what was creating this problem with downtime. That led us to discover a culture of insecurity about the work the individuals were doing. Due to inexperience or uncertainty, they were not clear about what they had to do next. They were constantly looking to leadership for direction. If the boss was not available at the right moment, everyone and everything tended to come to a halt.

Downtime is a very clear-cut measurement because you see it. If a worker is standing there, not doing anything, that is downtime. For my client, the metric of downtime was an easy way to measure his relative success at improving communication. It also then started the process of discovery as to what could be done to make sure downtime was reduced or eliminated.

## Outcomes Lead the Way to Measures

The thing I stress with leaders I coach is that it is your responsibility to come up with the results, the outcomes that you want, and get crystal-clear about what those outcomes should be. From there, put it on your people to figure out the process to get to those outcomes. That is essentially what I did with the manufacturing client in my example. We dug deeper and found out what he really wanted, which was zero downtime. Okay, if zero downtime is what you are hoping to create, what is preventing you from it? Once you have identified the factors getting in your way, how tangible are they? If they are too intangible to measure, what tangible evidence can you equate them to, in order to measure progress at removing those factors? That is where you will find the measures that matter in your unique situation.

The answers will depend on the size and scope of the particular organization. If you are thinking from a CEO level of a medium to large corporation, the things that you are looking at measuring are likely to be accounting measures that show up on financial statements, primarily sales and profits. If you are not achieving your sales and profit goals, then you should be digging into the potential causes of that shortfall.

This is where you have to be very careful to analyze the company from a holistic point of view. In many organizations, the attitude is that if sales are going down, well, that is a problem in the sales department. Fix that. These companies are just treating the symptoms, not the underlying problem. While there might be a problem in the sales department, is that because of the salespeople, or is it because of the people managing the sales force, or is it because of the marketing department—perhaps the salespeople do not have the right tools and supports for their sales process? Is it because of the company culture? Has the culture become one of, "we are order takers," as opposed to going out and actively seeking new business? Only a holistic analysis will reveal all components feeding into to the symptom revealed by a particular measure such as a sales goal.

## Metrics as Diagnostic Tools

A mediocre doctor will treat symptoms. He is prone to work at the level of the presenting symptom, "Your back hurts, therefore, I'm going to give you medication to take care of that back pain." A really good doctor will dig in to figure out, is the back pain because of the posture issue? Is it because of a nerve in another part of the body that is triggering pain in the back? Obviously the holistic, investigative approach that considers the whole body as an integrated system is going to produce better results long-term than simply treating systems as they appear.

You have to take the same approach in your own business. If sales are not meeting targets then yes, maybe there is a problem in your sales process, or maybe it's something else. Unfortunately, if you hire a sales consultant, he is likely to say, "Yes, sales are the problem," and then go in there and treat the symptom. Maybe he will uncover the real issue and come up with a fix, but more likely he will not. You have to treat every challenge or issue within your organization as something that may originate anywhere throughout your entire organization. Otherwise, your fixes will just achieve a short-term change that will probably fail to have a long-term effect on the issue that was the problem in the first place.

Metrics will help you diagnose where the problem is impacting your business. Three to five measures for each department or functional area should be enough to present warning signs to alert you to specific symptoms, so that you can investigate the holistic relationship of various symptoms to the actual root problem.

### Data Prioritization

The challenge with any kind of organizational measurement is avoiding data overload. I can think of a number of organizations that I have worked with where reams and reams of reports were produced. The leaders were expected to go through it all. You had to constantly analyze all this data. It is extremely difficult to track that much information.

A more effective approach is to boil the data down to three to five trackable measures that are critical indicators of how daily functions are operating. When those measures are on target, you will know that the outcomes at the end of the year will be what you want.

I have a client who loves gathering data and creating reports. If allowed, he would have a report and be collecting data for every little item. The reality is, there are only a couple of factors he truly needs to measure to know if he is successful at what he is doing or not. He needs a measure of financial performance related to his business statements, and he needs a measure of sales performance, such as the number of referrals he is getting from his clients and staff.

In any company, as you dig into each department and each layer of management, there are different metrics that the work group is responsible for that they need to measure. It should be no more than three to five measures. These measures do not need to roll up to higher levels of management. You do not need every department tracking every other department.

You worry about your measures. Let other functions worry about theirs. At the executive team level, the leaders are responsible for making sure each group's measures are tracking the behaviors or actions needed to stay aligned with the company's overall Path and Direction. At the department level, managers should be watching the three to five measures that indicate the outcomes their department is trying to achieve. We are looking at the micro cultures in each functional group. The organization is unified by the type of people given leadership roles, and how they go about managing. From there, each is autonomous, responsible for their individual results within their group.

## Leading Indicators and Lagging Indicators

Leading indicators are the tools you use going into a situation to determine what actions should be taken. Leading indicators help you plan ahead.

Lagging indicators are the measures that let you know if you have been doing things right. For example, say your expectation is that sales will go up by 10 percent. How will you know that you have been successful? If your sales go up by 10 percent or greater, that is proof you have done the right things to achieve the growth you were after. But you are not finding that out until well after the fact, when the lagging indicators come in. It is not giving you information you can steer by.

Most of us should spend equal time looking at leading indicators and lagging indicators. When your financial statement indicates whether you have been profitable or not in the last period, you are getting that information after the fact. You have already earned the revenue. You have already spent the money. The difference between revenue and expenses is either a positive or a negative number. It does not help you evaluate where to go; it reports the relative success of your past strategic choices. Too often, companies are looking at lagging indicators, such as sales history.

**KNOW THIS**

### Focus on Behaviors or Actions?

*Focusing on behaviors can be just as important as focusing on actions. Define and track positive behaviors, as these are often leading indicators of accomplishments to come.*

I recommend that you put your focus on leading indicators, and tie the outcome you want to the leading indicator that you can measure. I wish I could just tell you which leading indicators to use for different types of businesses, but that is a tough one to answer. You could take two businesses in the same industry and each is going to have its own specific leading indicators, based on that company's direction. It really can come down to a unique model for each company.

Sales trends can be a leading indicator because they reflect what is happening over a period of time. When the sales trend line quits pointing up and starts leveling out, it is a good indicator you need to pay attention. Anytime you start seeing that crest of the hill, you are either approaching a plateau and you are going to have to find a way to work through that, or you are receiving an early signal that sales are going to start dropping. It is a warning sign that the next trend is downward. Unfortunately most businesses do not take action until they are already on the downward slope, which makes the sales trend harder to correct. If sales trends shift from rising to falling, work backward to deduce the reason. Did you make a change to your sales process, product, or service? If you make a change, and sales begin to decline, you should be able to trace your steps back to the change.

### Leading Indicators: Worth the Work to Identify

*Leading indicators can be harder to find because so often their measurement comes after the fact. Take customer experience. The behaviors exhibited in a customer interaction could be an example of a leading indicator. The behavior is the desired response that triggers the lagging indicator, which could be an increase in referral business. Look at what behaviors or actions drive your desired outcomes.*

**KNOW THIS**

You have seen this happen time and time again, right? A company grows like gangbusters early on. A few years go by and there is still solid growth. Then all of the sudden, the company reaches a point where the growth from year four to year five flattens out. Instead of 8 percent to 10 percent as in the past, growth is now 2 percent to 3 percent. And then the next year is about equal to that. The company has hit this top of the hill. The cause could be any number of things, internal or external to the company. It can be driven by the economy. It can be driven by competition. It can be driven by internal culture, growing so fast that people were promoted out of their skill sets and never retrained for the skills needed in their new roles.

If you grew by 10 percent every year, but your growth has been flat this year, you have been given a signal that your market is changing. If your market is changing, so is your business. You need to change something about it.

Most businesses wait too long to make a change. If you wait until you are losing market share, it is very difficult to generate an immediate turnaround at that point. Everything takes time. When businesses are starting to lose market share or experience declining sales, it is definitely more difficult to make changes and get the business back to growing.

That is usually where I get called in as a consultant. A business will call after the fact and I will need to coach them through some repair work that should have been done two, three or five years earlier. But they do not act until whatever has changed is causing such a problem that it is really impacting their business.

Identifying a leading indicator related to sales is more difficult than you might think. For an example, let's go back to the manufacturing company I was working with on better communications. When they contacted me, they were looking for a sales or marketing person to help them fix their problem, which they had identified as a sales problem. Yes, they needed help with sales, but their approach was, "We need new marketing materials because we are not closing enough business."

In my work with them, I discovered their biggest challenge was not the fact that they were not writing enough proposals. In fact, they were writing more than enough proposals. That was not the issue.

It was not that they needed better collateral material, either. The problem was really the fact that they did not have a functioning sales force. Their people were not out selling anything. The company had gone from some good years when they could just turn on the lights in the building, the phone would ring and there would be as many orders as they could handle. But now, they were seeing increased competition. And with that competition, prices were starting to get driven down. The economy was starting to tighten up as well. What this sales force had done in the past was definitely not going to work in a tighter, more competitive, marketplace.

As we dug into it, the realization sank in that the marketing materials were not going to change anything. There was not enough of a relationship between the sales force and the customer. You can send out all the marketing materials you want. It is not going to build new relationships like an effective sales force will.

That company had crested the hill. There were leading indicators saying, "certain things are going pretty well here," but on balance, there were lagging indicators saying "sales may still be pretty strong, but we are not seeing growth like before. We are also seeing our customers getting more price-sensitive than in the past."

---

### Is Writing Proposals a Leading Indicator? Not Really.

*It would seem that proposal activity makes a good leading indicator because it points to where your next sales are likely to come from, and how much. I would recommend caution about that. In most cases I see doing proposals means the business is already there. The focus is on what exactly the deliverables and processes will be. I do not consider writing proposals to be positive sales work. Customer inquiries are a better leading indicator than sales proposals.*

**KNOW THIS**

---

Price sensitivity can be a leading indicator as it was in this case. When this company called in consultants, the sales volume was not as high as it had been. The competition was getting stronger. The price they could get for materials, which in this case was measured by the cubic yard, was dropping. Sales were still strong, but the warning signs had definitely started coming in. The leaders in that company thought the problem was that they did not have new, fresh-looking marketing material to support their sales. I was the only person interviewed who did not come at them with a proposal for a new brochure or website. I said, "You can scrap all that. Here's where I see your problem. A new website isn't going to change that."

This example shows why it is so important to find the right indicators, and why what makes up the "right" information is unique to each particular business.

## Data Mining

At this point data mining comes into the picture. Data mining is a knowledge discovery process that involves analyzing data from different perspectives and summarizing it into useful information. You have to look at all your available data, really lay it all out, and from there, prioritize the three to five indicators that yield the knowledge you need to track, function by function across the company, to keep every process and person aligned with the right day-to-day outcomes. Achieve those, and you are pretty much guaranteed to stay on the right path.

Where are the sources of data in your company? Once you start looking, you will find indicators everywhere—finance, marketing, production, and personnel matters. Let's zoom in for a closer look at each.

### Financial Data

The accountants produce the financial data. They look at the numbers from a dollars-and-cents perspective. That is a very important view because there are lots of leading indicators you can find in sales and in expenses. But that should not be all you look at.

Sure, having an accountant look at your books and make recommendations about what you should do is very valuable. Because accountants are strictly looking at dollars and cents, it's very easy for them to say, "You know what? If you cut your costs here, lessen your expenses over there, you will be more profitable."

That may be true but it may or may not be the right course of action. Consider what happens if you are in a growth mode. Nobody has ever grown by strictly cutting expenditures. Make sure your accountants know your full business plan, your view of the Direction, Path, People, Processes and Measures to be sure they are aware of all the other factors affecting your strategy besides dollars-and-cents performance.

### Sales

The sales element represents a lot more than just the dollars and cents produced by invoices. Sales data worth monitoring should focus on leading indicators—activity such as where you are prospecting, how prospects are moving through the sales funnel, how much business you are closing. What would happen if you closed a higher percentage of business? Those are sales metrics that that can be valuable.

### Production

Production metrics include measures of output, such as quality and error ratios. You can measure process improvements, such as increases in efficiency. You can put a metric to innovation. You could actually compartmentalize innovation in and of it because innovation is the risk-taking aspect of your business. Typically, the costs there are much higher. The return in some cases may be lower in the short term, but what you are doing with innovation is trying to springboard into a new product, a new service, a new system that is going to launch you out ahead of your competitors. Innovation is so important to being a Golden Apple company, achieving true competitive differentiation that it is absolutely worth monitoring, if you can identify the tangible output that equates to true innovation day-to-day. Failing to incorporate innovation into daily operations is where many businesses fail to grow. This is where they run into trouble. They get so risk-averse; they do not want to stick their neck out anywhere. They become victims of the environment that surrounds them. You have got to be ready to take the risk of putting some expenditure toward innovation.

### *Personnel*

There are several data points to consider in the personnel area. Depending on your organization, the top three to five indicators will vary, but in any organization, you should always look at turnover. The higher degree of turnover you have the stronger the sign that there is a potential cultural problem brewing.

That is because turnover comes about, in most cases, because somebody believes that his needs are not being satisfied in your organization. That becomes either a hiring issue or a leadership issue. If you are hiring the wrong people, you are going to have turnover. If you are not leading your people correctly, you are going to have turnover.

How you measure the degree of innovation in your company can be a personnel management issue, and it can reveal whether you are staying on the right path. Do people bring new ideas forward? Are those people empowered to research those ideas to see what is feasible? You could find a tangible indicator for those.

Another aspect of the personnel function worth measuring is retention and application of a new learning. What is going on with learning and development in your company? All too often it is left to the individual to figure out a personal development plan. They make their own choices about learning opportunities, and no one holds them accountable for retaining or applying what they learned afterward. There is no follow-up. Ideally, companies pay attention to how development applies to a person's role and future career path, but too often, I see the opposite. Training is just a hodge-podge with no clear plan for individuals in terms of where they are going in the future and what tools they need to develop in order to get there. That is where people sign up for seminars, attend day-long or weekend retreats. They spend hundreds if not thousands of the company's dollars, supposedly to learn new skill sets, and then walk away never really being able to apply any of it.

The right way to use training is to get a clear picture of where each individual wants to go, and get a clear understanding of how that fits in to the organization's Path.

People need purpose. Without purpose, people will do what they need to do in a job to get by, and that's all. They become the clock-punchers. If a better opportunity comes along, the grass looks greener somewhere else, they are the first to jump ship. You have to look at creating a process around developing people that is going to produce a return on investment. You should be able to measure what that return on investment is.

The leaders I know struggle with this. The rational side says, "Training is necessary. We should be doing it in any economy." The emotional side responds out of fear. "The economy is going down. I need to save money any way I can. Training is an easy cost to cut because I cannot measure whether cuts make an impact on my organization."

I think there are indicators you can monitor that show where there is an ROI on that investment in training. It takes more of a conscious effort and it takes more work by the leadership team, but if the leaders are doing the right things, letting the staff take care of problems as they arise and staying focused on the growth of the organization and the growth of the individuals, there will be ROI. You have got data you can manage by in your measures of retention and application of new learning, as well.

To develop measures of ROI for training, identify what the desired outcome of training will be. Determine what behaviors are lacking. It may not be an information issue, but an attitude issue.

So far, we have been considering the internal metrics that give feedback on every aspect of your operation— finance performance, sales, production and personnel. I have counseled you to keep your eye on leading indicators because these allow you to be more nimble than lagging indicators. So far, our focus has been on the inner circle, the internal influences that you can control. Now, let's turn our focus to the outer circle. What is going on in the external environment?

### External Environmental Measures

External measures can be found in economic performance and competitive intelligence.

Externally, the stock market is an important indicator of trends because any sort of positive or negative change in government, international law, trade relationships or other corporate structure causes almost immediate impact on the economy through the stock market. Your focus should not be on the specific spikes, the ups and downs, but the trends between those ups and downs. Is the trend line arching up even though there might be spikes that are higher and spikes that are lower? Or is it leveling off or heading down?

Another important indicator is your competition. What are they doing? You want to know, not so you can follow what they are doing, but so you can leapfrog what they are working on and land ahead of the pack. Gathering competitive intelligence is one approach.

Figure out what they are doing and how they are doing it, so you can identify what makes you different, discover opportunities they have not seen that could give you an advantage.

Another external measure is the political environment, at the local, regional, and national level. Where are the trends going?

Consumer trends are another important indicator to follow. What is the consumer going to desire next? Some companies have been really good at predicting what consumers will need in the future.

### *Risk It or Lose It*

*As much as we might like to say we are risk-takers, many people are not. Particularly in times of recession, when* KNOW THIS *people are feeling like their options are limited, they lose their appetite for risk. In fact, recession can be the best opportunity because, if you look at the trending mindset, everyone else is in the mode of cutback, reserve cash, and just get by. Some people actually put themselves into recessionary mode because of their fears. You can talk yourself into being so cautious and slow that you end up just like everybody else. By now you should know that is a pitfall.*

Apple has innovated products that create demand, instead of creating a product that fills an existing demand. You have got to ask, "What is going to place me, not just level with my competition, but beyond them?" I know that's not easy. The moment you do leap out ahead, your investment of resources, and your exposure to risk, all tend to go up significantly. But failing to innovate too often leaves companies in a "me-too" position, stuck in the middle of the pack.

There are a lot of simple behavioral changes you can make within your company culture in response to external environmental measures that could make a dramatic impact on your growth. These do not have to come with a huge price tag. Find them or risk losing your competitive difference and all the advantages that go with true differentiation.

## Accountability

I have given you a lot of data points, potential measures for the different functional areas in your business. Now you need to figure out how these data points relate to the people who are responsible for what is going on in each of those areas. It is critical that the indicators you monitor are not something that a leader alone can measure. The data points need to be accessible to the people who are accountable for them.

If you have a sales team and you are not giving them the right data as soon as it's available, they either have to come to you to ask for the information or wait until you get around to handing the information to them. That sales team ends up steering by a lagging indicator because of the delay in getting the data they need. That team could think they are doing everything right and then three months later they get the report saying, "Well, no, you actually missed it by 10 percent." Without timely data, very little control and very little true measurement can go on.

Accessibility of the data is important because, if I am responsible for something and I cannot check to see how I am doing at any point I think its necessary, how can I be held accountable for it?

Instead, I am relying on somebody else to feed me that information, which means someone else is more accountable for my work than I am. As a consultant I see this time and time again. The tools used to measure and track don't float down to the people who actually need that information.

Measures give you the feedback you need to steer effectively and efficiently toward your goals. They will help you correct your course if you are beginning to wander. They will help you spot problems ahead so you can chart a new course. Measures are worth getting right, as much as any other aspect of your business we have talked about.

Identify the right data points to give you the indicators you need for your particular business. Work with your leadership team to identify the three to five leading indicators that allow each function to hit its marks, day by day. Internal indicators will give you information about financial performance, sales activity, production, and personnel. External indicators will help you see trends in the environment and with your competitors and customers. Choose leading indicators, to keep your operation nimble.

Find the right measures, and get them automatically into the hands of the people who are accountable for them, and you are on your way toward true competitive differentiation.

## Conclusion

Now you are familiar with the five tasks that, when given the attention of your leadership team, will make yours a company with the culture of a Golden Apple. I have made the case that creating that culture will lead to increased profits, lower costs, greater stability, and easier recruiting. Are you ready to commit to the Five Tasks of the Golden Apple?

# PART 3

## Start Now

# You're On Your Way

Many chapters ago I mentioned the comedian who said, "I want to be different just like everyone else!" Everybody wants to be an individual and recognized as such. The comedian wants to be enough like everyone else to be familiar and non-threatening, but different enough to stand out as an entertainer. For a comedian, that is an achievable goal. The challenge for business is the same—to be recognized for its uniqueness, but not so far out there that customers cannot clearly understand what they sell. To succeed, both a comedian and a business need to create a sustainable advantage through competitive differentiation.

For a comedian or a business, knowing something about human psychology is an asset that can contribute to achieving that goal of true differentiation.

## You Must Overcome Compartmentalization

People need to compartmentalize the things they think about. People have a need to put things in a box, to define what those things are. That is where the whole "apples to apples" metaphor comes from. That need to say, "This fits in Category X, so I can relate it to everything I already know about Category X." When I am talking to people about new concepts, if I cannot find a way to relate it to something they already understand, it's very difficult for them to follow where I am going.

This is supported by brain science around learning theory. You have to attach new learning to existing learning. It is very difficult to remember or make sense of that new knowledge without a category to assign it to.

Many businesses struggle with this. They want to become more than what they are perceived as by their consumers. A bank, a dentist, a retail location—the category does not matter, the dilemma is there.

A lot of the businesses I speak with offer a service, and their clients see them for that service alone. I can even relate to this myself. When I first started my own business, the consulting my first clients hired me for was sales coaching. My miscalculation was that I was selling a product—the training. That is what got me into trouble because when the need for the product went away, so did the need for me. In the beginning I was selling materials, not my experience—not what made me different. I got lucky. I learned from my mistakes and was able to rebound in a very difficult economic environment. Through this experience came self discovery, which led to making the changes I did. Those strategic changes have resulted in a consulting practice with long-term clients who continue to refer business my way.

When you are new in business, you take whatever comes your way. But that can have long-lasting ramifications for your business. When you are starting out you are trying to feed your family and a good opportunity comes along—you take it. As your business grows—if it grows—you realize that you will have to make choices about the market you will serve and the services you will offer. By

**KNOW THIS**

### Be the Best or Be the Cheapest?

*If no option is clearly the best, most people will buy the cheapest. That is what leads to price competition and commoditization. Most companies wish to be perceived as the best, but few actually take the actions necessary to become the best. The rest of the companies suffer in purgatory competing on price and fighting each other over whatever they can get. Are you doing the work it takes to achieve the status of "clearly the best"?*

now you can probably say it with me: "Try to be all things to all people and you'll end up being nothing to nobody."

Once I realized I needed to differentiate my consulting business, it was just a matter of figuring out what to specialize in. I was back to asking myself what am I really good at, just as I had been in the beginning. What was it that I am best at? What was going to make me different?

For me, the answer centered around the strategy with the emphasis on follow-through—getting people to use it. There are plenty of strategic planners out there. But there are few who go beyond that and take the client into a process of executing the plan. That is where I saw a great need that dovetailed with my own strengths. Plenty of firms get a strategic plan and never do anything with it. That was a differentiator for me.

But even that was not specific enough to allow me to communicate my message—what differentiates me. By luck, about that time I happened to be referred to a bank. I was told in that referral that my services would be a good fit for the financial services industry. Until that point I had no experience in banking. Some people would see that as a detriment but I saw it as an advantage. I would be able to ask questions that someone familiar with banking would not think to ask. I would bring ideas that are fresh to that industry because I had been working outside it.

In a similar way, I developed expertise in specializing in the health care sector. And lately, I have been leveraging those strengths to move into globalization strategies. I am helping business leaders build relationships in China.

The point of relating my experience is to say that you must differentiate on a factor that is central to your core strengths, and meaningful to the consumer. Then communicate that difference with a compelling message that conveys how whatever you offer moves buyers from pain to pleasure. Work with that human psychology, the tendency toward compartmentalization and grouping that people do. Make sure you stand out.

Everything I have talked about in Part 2 of this book, the Five Tasks of the Golden Apple, boils down to a plan of action for standing out, becoming a Golden Apple among all the reds in the barrel.

I challenge you to put these recommendations into action starting now. Spend some quality time on Direction, Path, People, Processes, and Measures with your leadership team. Then revisit the Reality Assessments in Chapter 2. I am confident you will see improvement in your scores—and your bottom line.

## For Those in Special Situations...

Now, I would like to offer some suggestions for the leaders in special situations who are reading this book. How do you maintain your attention on the Five Tasks of the Golden Apple when you are in one of the following situations: start-up mode, experiencing high growth or dealing with a maturity that is starting to feel like stagnation?

### The Start-up Stage

When businesses are starting out, there is a real tendency to want to be all things to all people. You think that saying "no" to a particular request will starve your company of the cash flow it requires to grow. This leads to a kind of corporate "Attention Deficit Disorder" I run into all too frequently in the business world today. Companies are battling for every dime and are afraid to let any opportunity pass them by. The answer is to prioritize your activity. Focus on the Direction you identified in your planning stage.

Probably the most critical decision facing the company in start-up mode is the question of who to hire. Too many entrepreneurs unknowingly end up hiring clones of them because that is who they feel comfortable with. They also wish to avoid conflict—a natural tendency. When we hire similar personalities, we eliminate certain forms of conflict. We also create new ones because now there are competing strengths and weaknesses.

If you have read Chapter 6 about the Third Task of the Golden Apple—People—you know that balance is essential. As the firm grows, you will need people who are action-oriented, social people to keep the group connected, analytics to mind the details raise the risk-management issues, and some persistent, thoughtful types who just put their shoulders against the wheel and get the job done. All these personalities contribute something to the organization that makes the whole stronger than the parts.

My best advice for you is to hire for attitudes, and not only for specific technical skills. If someone has the right attitude you can teach, him or her, the technical skills. And do not hire people who just make you comfortable because they are similar to you.

### The High-Growth Stage

The problem most businesses wish they face is being too busy. When you have that problem, you are probably in high-growth mode. But success can kill a business faster than you realize. There may be plenty of cash coming in, from investors or sales, or there may be a cash flow shortage created by expanding payroll and inventory required to deliver as the company grows. Too much cash can lead to poor hiring decision--just filling gaps to try and get more work done. Too little cash can impact customer service, by creating delays or employee morale, if meeting payroll becomes a stretch—and either will stop that high-growth stage in its tracks.

If cash flow is not the source of problems, leadership may be. High growth requires leaders who are willing to allow people to do their jobs. Mitigate risk as much as possible but coach your people and let them make their own decisions with your guidance.

Without effective distribution of control, the organization can seize up faster than an engine burning oil. The danger is that a business that is growing too fast will not be able to optimize the aspects that brought on that growth. When I was working as a manager in a fast-growing company, I would tell people that I would rather run shorthanded with the right people than have to address the needs of having enough bodies but the wrong ones.

Leadership is hard enough. It only gets more complicated when you have a wrong fit with personnel. The leaders must stay attuned to the Five Tasks of the Golden Apple, and that can only happen if the staff is good at their technical roles and above all, bring the right attitude to the job. This is why it is so important to create an environment where you are the employer of choice, so that leaders can let go of minutiae and really lead.

### The Maturity Stage

When a company has achieved maturity, processes tend to take priority over people. This is the company where people say, "we've always done it that way," and that may be the first sign of problems to come. One clue that your company is approaching a maturity that might be leading to stagnation is if the talent pool does not seem the same. Are you still able to attract top talent? People are not as attracted to work for a company that is seen as stagnant. They want to be involved in something that is growing, exciting, innovative.

If this describes your company, I would emphasize that it's time to review the Fourth Task of the Golden Apple: pay attention to your processes. As you seek out ways to remove inefficiency, you are apt to discover ways to bring new innovations into the mix. That next product or service might be the one that puts you back in the mind-set and growth potential of the start-up or high-growth firm.

## What's Your Legacy?

For any business leader, the ultimate question is—when you leave, what will happen to the organization? If you have done your job well, the company is prepared to operate successfully going forward, after you have left. The CEO who hires a replacement who can hit the ground running has done a great service to the firm he leaves behind. This is the ultimate moment to hire on attitude, not technical skills.

Jim Collins, author of *Good to Great*, encourages leaders to ask themselves, "What are your core values? What is your core purpose, beyond just making money?" These are questions that will help you make the transition from leader to your Next Big Thing.

If you have accomplished the Five Tasks of the Golden Apple, you have built a company with a sustainable competitive difference, the ability to innovate, efficient processes including a process for continuous improvement, and a balanced, high-functioning leadership team. If you were called away tomorrow, this company is going to maintain its direction. Not only that, its leadership is experienced in the Five Tasks that helped it achieve the high level of functioning of a Golden Apple company. In time the cycle will continue, with strategic planning concerning Direction, Path, People, Processes, and Measures. This company can adapt and change to maintain its competitive differentiation.

That's a good place to be. So give each of the Five Tasks the attention it deserves, and when you finish the fifth? Start over at the first. That is the art of being a Golden Apple.

Look for other books and training materials by Dan Paulson, including the workbook that accompanies *Apples to Apples: How to Stand Out from Your Competition.*

*www.invisionbusinessdevelopment.com/store*